MICHELE KAMBOLIS

GENERATION
STRESSED

PLAY-BASED TOOLS
TO HELP YOUR CHILD
OVERCOME ANXIETY

PUBLISHED BY LIFETREE MEDIA

Published by
LifeTree Media Ltd.
www.lifetreemedia.com

Distributed by
Greystone Books Ltd.
www.greystonebooks.com

Cataloguing data available from Library and Archives Canada
ISBN 978-0-9936530-0-1 (paperback)
ISBN 978-0-9936530-1-8 (epub)
ISBN 978-1-928055-03-7 (pdf)

Editing by Maggie Langrick
Cover design by Naomi MacDougall
Cover photograph by Stephanie Rausser / Trunk Archive
Interior design by Ingrid Paulson
Interior artwork by Kezzia Crossley
Printed and bound in Canada by Friesens

LifeTree Media Ltd. is committed to reducing the
consumption of old-growth forests in the books
it publishes. This book is one step towards that goal.

Dedicated to my children
Alex & Stamos

They are my biggest teachers
of the power of presence and connection

"How do we communicate worthiness to our children? Only through our presence, our full-on, engaged attuned presence."

DR. SHEFALI TSABARY

CONTENTS

INTRODUCTION

The School Run

It's Wednesday morning, but you're already longing for the weekend. You get the kids up, pack the lunches. Your daughter can't find socks. Your son won't put down the iPad. There's no time for breakfast. A protein bar will have to do. Your daughter freaks out; she forgot her gym clothes. You get the kids to school in the nick of time, but now you're late for work again. You're stressed, the kids are stressed and life feels out of control.

And that's just the beginning of your day. The school calls to tell you your son is sick. He sat down to take a test and couldn't breathe, and now he won't stop crying. You take him to the doctor. Has he been sleeping well? No. Has he had stomachaches or headaches? Yes. How long has this been going on? Weeks, if not months. Yes, you've been worried but you hoped it would pass. It hasn't.

Aggression, perfectionism, sleeplessness, clinginess, stomachaches, nightmares—all are telling us one thing: kids are stressed. The American Psychological Association's 2014 *Stress in America* study sums it up: almost one-third of teens say their stress is on the rise and most believe it'll only get worse. And teens aren't the only ones affected. The insidious effects of stress can be seen in the very young—20 percent of school-age children have a diagnosable

1

mental disorder. That's one in five! If it seems that life for kids today is more stressful than when we were growing up, that's because it is. Our hurried, harrowed culture demands that kids compete, perform and excel, even as it places bleeping, blinking distractions in front of them at every turn. We see the pressure children are under and we wonder how they can possibly cope, let alone thrive. The answer, too often, is that they can't. External stress breeds internal anxiety, which in turn shows up in the bodies and behavior of kids in myriad ways, some of which are hard to read.

Fact: All children worry, holding on to an average of eight worries at a time. The children who worry the least tend to be boys in fourth grade.

Many children are checked out, more easily bored than ever before and unable to fill the time between their periods of busyness. Today when most children enter my counseling room, they seem disoriented and unsure of what to do with the toys. It isn't long before they ask, "Do you have computer games here?" They seem less curious; instead, they're waiting to be told what comes next. Their wide-eyed wonder has been replaced by the vacant stare of screen time. Other kids are highly sensitive and easily overwhelmed by the real and imagined threats they see everywhere. From spiders to spelling tests, the world for these children contains many perils.

Many of us who care for children feel we are at a loss, fearing that maybe we aren't firm enough, understanding enough or somehow skilled enough to find a solution to their struggles. We take the latest parenting workshops and bolster our kids with sports and tutoring, hoping to build them up so they can engage with the world with confidence. But stress is not something kids should simply get used to. Eating a steady diet of junk food as a youngster doesn't help the body adapt to it, it makes it sicker. It's the same with stress. And as with any negative habit, the pattern sticks until we break the cycle.

We are up against a great deal in caring for our kids. A culture of disconnection, self-importance and greed constantly challenges our instinctive efforts to cultivate in them a sense of safety and well-being. Whether I'm meeting with a child who's terrified to go to school, working with a parent fatigued by years of battling a child's anxiety or helping my own children navigate their difficult moments, I too have to search for the language and emotional presence of mind that will create openings for real change. Like any parent, there are times when I struggle to soothe separation anxiety or relieve my child's unbearable weight of worry. But as parents and caregivers we need to learn how to accept and manage our own stress levels and anxiety so we can be truly present for our children, allowing them to sense that they are felt, seen and accepted in their own strength and vulnerability. As the great teacher and developmental psychologist Gordon Neufeld said at a conference recently, "Have your child's heart and you will shield them from a wounding world."

Ultimately, this book is not about fixing children or shaping their behavior. It is about using your caring and dependable presence to be there with them, for them, showing caring and using that connection to help them find a way out of debilitating and chronic anxiety. The tools in this book can be great aids, but the message goes far beyond remedial measures. By tuning in to our children's needs, we're helping them to become resilient, connected and strong.

For children whose anxiety is at a clinical level, we wisely turn to the expertise of mental health professionals. But the factor that makes the biggest difference for kids in applying their new coping skills is parental involvement. A therapist will spend only one to two hours per week with a child, leaving the other 166 hours for us to connect with, support and teach our children the skills they need to thrive. In other words, our unwavering presence matters. The activities, exercises and tools laid out in this book aren't prescriptive; instead, they encourage opportunities for children to discover their tender and sometimes scary feelings and naturally begin to lean into them. By providing reassurance and strategies, we help them to understand and regulate their thoughts and feelings. And they will learn that their vulnerability is respected, that it is possible to accept fear and that by doing so they can allow it to move through them.

I've had the privilege to work for almost two decades as a child and family therapist. Through CHI Kids, a community- and school-based program developed in my practice, thousands of children and their parents have found relief from anxiety using the same play-based tools described in this book. These activities are drawn from the traditions of cognitive behavior therapy (CBT), positive psychology and interpersonal neurobiology. CBT helps people understand the relationship between thoughts, feelings and behavior; positive psychology is the scientific study of those qualities and choices that help people to thrive and build a positive future outlook; interpersonal neurobiology examines the mind, the body and the brain and emphasizes thoughts and feelings of compassion, kindness and well-being for ourselves and the people around us. In practice, picture classrooms filled with children breathing mindfully, squeezing out tension with progressive relaxation exercises and blowing their negative, irrational beliefs into a balloon and letting it go. I've had the joy of witnessing many of the tender, healing moments these activities can foster between a child and a caring adult.

While these activities are supported by science, this is less a "how-to" book than a "how-to-be" book. No matter how skilled we become in mastering tools for communication and relaxation or confronting irrational beliefs, what's most essential to cultivate the space for learning is a strong, open and compassionate relationship with our kids. This is one of the first lessons I learned, and it is still one of the most important.

In my early days as a newly practicing clinician, I was president of the BC Association for Play Therapy. In that capacity, I got to know and benefitted from the wisdom of such brilliant speakers as Viola Brody (*The Dialogue of Touch*), Dr. John Allan (*Inscapes of the Child's World*) and Dr. Jane Garland (*Taming Worry Dragons*). Eighteen years ago they spoke about the importance of mindfulness, not because it was the trendiest parenting concept—in fact, this was years before the parenting movement hit its stride—but because their research and personal wisdom told them acceptance through moment-by-moment awareness of thoughts, feelings, bodily sensations and surrounding environment is essential for healing.

At one conference, I attended a keynote address given by Viola Brody. She knew that caring touch and nurturing physical affection are essential to a child's healthy development. She also understood that if parents are to have the ability to meet this essential need, mindfulness is key. As the conference participants gathered in the room for her speech, she invited us all to do something groundbreaking—to touch one another. There I sat, holding hands with a group of strangers, eyes closed, simply noticing my own awareness and my connection with others. We sat for what felt like an inordinate amount of time, and then something magical happened—I let go. And in the letting go came an experience of oneness that was palpable. I knew this was the healing, connected experience that every child must have in order to be whole.

After meeting Viola and acting as her young and eager tour guide around town, I continued to correspond with her for years until her death in 2003. In the latter years she wasn't always able to recall who I was, but that didn't seem to matter—her caring and generosity were unwavering. Viola would have been 94 when she wrote her final letter to me, saying: "I've slowed down quite a bit but I'm still working with families—they need a lot of support. I'm so happy for you to share my work with others . . . it's meant to be shared." And so I share it with you.

THIS BOOK DIRECTLY addresses parents and caregivers but its message is the same for teachers, grandparents, clinicians and anyone else doing the vital work of nurturing children. My goal is to help you use the power of your relationship as a catalyst to help the children in your life grow into themselves, resilient and whole. And while we'll take a look at a variety of well-supported practical approaches, we'll continue to come back to that original goal—to help our children thrive through our steady presence.

Fact: A whopping 44% of youth between ages 8 and 17 describe having sleeping problems related to anxiety and stress, and the parents of only 13% of those children are aware of the issue.

While working towards making these life-changing shifts in the quality of your relationship, and in your kids' (and your) mindset and actions, it's important to have realistic expectations. You'll have setbacks and times when you'll wonder whether the attachment-centered activities will actually have the effect you're looking for. Some of the tools will appear simple, and you'll wonder how something as basic as changing your breathing or squeezing your muscles could possibly address the stubborn anxiety our children face. After all, by now you've probably tried a whole host of approaches, hopeful at the onset of each one, only to be disappointed by a weak result. I encourage you to keep an open mind and persevere—there is power in the simplicity of living consciously. Throughout, I've also included many personal stories drawn from my experience with my clients. While identifying details have been changed to maintain their privacy, their compelling stories are very real and may offer you insight and encouragement in working with your own kids.

We'll talk about the causes of childhood stress and anxiety, their effects on learning and relationships and the reasons that anxiety is so relentlessly on the rise. We'll discuss the myths and misunderstandings about childhood anxiety and the ways in which it is commonly misinterpreted; for example, as behavioral disorder or hyperactivity. You'll learn that accepting our children's discomfort opens the way for them to acknowledge what is showing up in their thoughts and emotions, and in turn to move through it and past it. You'll come to better understand the role the brain plays in their distress and more objectively engage in a dialogue with the negative irrational beliefs so intent on crowding out our children's joy and curiosity.

You'll learn play-based exercises developed in my clinical practice, in CHI Kids school and in community-based anxiety-reduction groups. These exercises are designed for children ages 6–12, but can be used with very young kids, older kids and even adults. You'll find out how to take CBT out of the therapy room and into your family home, boosting its effects with the power and spirit of your parent-child attachment.

Finally, we'll talk about healthy, effective ways to manage anxiety and buffer our children against life's challenges, from finding support from the right mental health professional if needed to making lifestyle changes, setting realistic goals and creating reasonable and health-based expectations. Your whole family will benefit as you learn a range of methods based on positive psychology to boost everyday happiness. By awakening to the power of our connection with our children and using science-based tools in a playful way, we can directly administer the antidote to "generation stressed" and restore a sense of joy in our children's lives, as well as our own.

ONE

INSIDE THE ANXIETY EPIDEMIC

Arianna

When I first met Arianna, she was the most withdrawn, unreachable child I had ever seen. She rarely met my gaze, and I knew I'd have to work hard to connect with her. When she spoke, her voice was flat and lifeless, and it seemed that her life force had been all but extinguished.

Her parents told me that as a fifth grader, Arianna had led an active life, playing soccer and hanging out with her friends, and they described her as having been a warm, sensitive and compliant child. Now, two years later, she seemed disengaged with life, spending time only with her twin sister and seldom joining her family for restaurant dinners or outings. Beneath her timidity were persistently racing thoughts, stomachaches and a dark foreboding that something terrible was about to happen.

She had seen "talk therapists" before, her parents told me, who had discussed at length all the underlying reasons for her distress—her parents' divorce, her eldest sister's move to a new school and her persistent struggle to feel "good enough." Arianna seemed to have great "understanding" about why she felt anxious, but talk therapy hadn't freed her from her emotional terror.

She wanted to have friends, go to the mall and finish seventh grade with her peers. She knew she was falling behind both academically and socially, but she was unable to leave the house, let alone challenge her fears about the wider world. And she knew that her parents were exasperated and angry that the time and effort they'd put into several different, well-meaning approaches had been essentially unsuccessful.

Nicholas

From very early on, Nicholas's mother could see he would be a challenging child to parent. The infant years were unbearable. He had a highly sensitive temperament and was terribly difficult to soothe; putting him down for more than a few moments was impossible. His pediatrician surmised that Nicholas must be experiencing some kind of chronic physical discomfort, or perhaps colic, but offered no solutions. When Nicholas entered grade school, his play dates were few and far between. He was easily agitated and often lashed out at other children. Even when he was able to hold it together at school, Nicholas returned home emotionally defensive and disconnected.

A pediatric psychiatrist diagnosed ADHD (attention deficit hyperactivity disorder) and prescribed stimulants, but the medication only seemed to make Nicholas more restless and sad. He'd had treatment using a biofeedback machine that identified how his body was reacting to stress and helped him try to manage those impulses, he'd been to play therapy to help him learn to express his anxiety using toys and art and his mother had pulled wheat gluten, dairy and sugar almost entirely from his diet. By the time Nicholas was eight years old, his mother had taken numerous parenting workshops, read dozens of books about parent-child relationships and dragged her husband to several child specialists to try to better understand their son. By the time she reached my office, she felt she was failing Nicholas and she was overcome with parental guilt. Yet, still Nicholas was suffering and was quick to say, "I hate my life. I wish I didn't exist!"

The anxiety epidemic

Anxiety has many faces. Some children worry excessively or are bombarded with their own negative thoughts; others have trouble eating or sleeping or become easily overwhelmed by a change in their routine. Anxiety can look like defiance, resistance or lack of focus. It is sometimes attributed to a shy temperament or minimized as a being "just a phase" or "no big deal." However, for parents witnessing their child struggle with these emotional challenges, anxiety most certainly is a big deal.

I, too, believe that childhood anxiety deserves our attention. After eighteen years of counseling children in schools, clinics and private practice, I've seen a startling increase in the frequency and seriousness of clinical levels of anxiety in children and youth. In fact, according to the Anxiety and Depression Association of America one in eight children today has a clinical level of anxiety. And when we factor in children with milder levels of anxiety, the number skyrockets. It is this cultural trend that this book addresses and that is leading experts and parents the world over to dub this era the Age of Anxiety.

Left unaddressed, chronic anxiety can disrupt many aspects of development, including a child's capacity to learn and ability to connect socially as well as the opportunity for the brain to grow and make connections. In time, children with high levels of anxiety are more likely to face depression, turn to substance use, become less likely to finish high school and may therefore have a harder time keeping a job or managing financially.

Fact: In the United States, anxiety disorders cost more than $42 billion each year in hospitalizations, disability disbursements, medical care and lost productivity.

To understand the role culture has played in this sharp generational rise in mental disorders, Jean Twenge of San Diego State University conducted one of the most groundbreaking studies to date. The 2004 study, published in *Personality and Social Psychology Review*, assessed data from ninety-seven studies to examine change over time in "locus of control." In psychology, we use the term "locus of control" to describe the causal relationship between our behavior and rewards. The locus of control can be either intrinsic (inside ourselves) or extrinsic (outside ourselves). It answers the question of who determines our fate: us or outside forces beyond our control. With an intrinsic locus of control, we determine our own priorities and are empowered to work towards them through our own efforts. In other words, our goals relate to our values, personal growth and relationships, and our self-esteem springs directly from our innate qualities. An intrinsic locus of control brings a sense of connectedness, community engagement, concern for the environment, and a desire to truly make a difference, which leads to greater happiness overall. It roots us in shared responsibility and enlivens our spirit.

With an extrinsic locus of control, in contrast, we believe our decisions and our lives are beyond our control, that our fate is out of our hands. This tends to bring a heightened focus on external goals, which often include status, money or fame, and on materialism, peer pressure and competitiveness, which wreak havoc on our values and priorities. Twenge looked at data from samples of typical children and college students as far back as 1960 and discovered something alarming: the scores showed that young people became substantially more directed by external forces between 1960 and 2002. The conclusions pointed towards a culture in crisis.

Despite advances in medicine, a better understanding of health and nutrition, an abundance of educational opportunity and greater financial resources for the average North American family, our children are suffering more than ever. But why? Twenge tells us the problem is in large part because we feel more alienated and cynical, while at the same time we've become progressively more outwardly focused, measuring our personal worth and success in life by our possessions and accomplishments. In other words, Twenge's study shows that we are increasingly placing our locus of control outside of our strongest place of power—ourselves.

Feeling that we don't have control over our decisions is one of the biggest contributors to stress and anxiety. If our sense of well-being is linked to unstable variables such as how many "likes" we have on our Facebook page or whether or not other people approve of our clothing, we abdicate any sense of control we might have over our well-being. So it's no surprise that as we've given up our intrinsic locus of control, our children and youth feel more hopeless and overwhelmed than they did over half a century ago.

Fact: Girls are twice as likely as boys to have an anxiety disorder in childhood, and this gender difference only increases with age.

This cultural shift in values hasn't happened overnight: Twenge's research and common sense tell us that we, parents and caregivers, are the original "Generation Stressed." The ego-driven culture of the '70s and '80s took a high spiritual and psychological toll on Generation X, leading to higher stress levels and a greater sense of isolation than in previous generations. Now stressed parents ourselves, many of us are raising stressed kids, our natural parenting instincts muffled by a society-wide decrease in interpersonal connection.

Polarized parenting

In response to this anxiety-driven culture, two forms of extreme parenting have emerged: push hard or pull back.

Punishments, rewards, confiscation, banishing, busying, bribes, incentives, threats, praise, warnings, goals, pleading and force are the tools of "push hard" parents. We try to shape behavior through a mix of positive and negative reinforcements to correct whatever we believe to be *wrong* within the child. In her book *Battle Hymn of the Tiger Mother,* author Amy Chua exemplifies this trend, writing openly about placing unyielding pressure on her child to succeed.

However, when children are only responding instinctively to force, they are not learning how to govern themselves. In fact, the more we force our kids, the more our bond with them becomes fractured and the more our threats and bribery interfere with the development of their natural independence. Once the rewards or the punishments stop, so too do the desired results. We misinterpret our children's behavior as an attempt to gain control and our stress level increases as our capacity for effective parenting decreases. At the same time, our children feel disconnected from us and start to become anxious. Caught up as we are in our own stress and emotional wounds, we are unable to draw our children towards us, soothe their anxiety and guide and enliven their growth.

Sweeping the path clear of all obstacles to banish failure from a child's life is the hallmark of "pull-back," or helicopter, parents. We do this for all kinds of reasons. We may believe we are helping our kids by preventing situations that may cause them stress and anxiety, or because we, ourselves, feel anxious or fear failure and want to spare our kids from possible criticism or reproach. Pull-back parents are reluctant to allow their children to walk to school independently, jump in to make sure homework is done "just right" and are quick to call the soccer coach if their child isn't getting enough time on the field.

Denied the opportunity to discover their own strength and resourcefulness in the face of challenges, children raised by helicopter parents grow more fearful of failure, less confident and more anxious. When these kids fail to become independent on their own, the parents' own anxiety rises and the parent-child bond is weakened. The forceful approach that goes hand in hand with helicopter parenting inhibits children's ability to feel open and safe as they attempt to process difficult situations through problem solving and understanding.

Both forms of extreme parenting draw intense criticism from a culture that places as much pressure on parents as it does on children. Undoubtedly, a healthier approach to parenting involves removing ourselves from this dichotomy altogether; however, I wish we could have a little more compassion for each other and realize that, misguided or not, we all do the best we can. Innately we all have the ability to first tune in to ourselves and then to the needs of our children. In this place, our parenting decisions are informed not by outside pressures but by who we are and how we need to respond to our children's individual temperament, strengths and needs. When kids feel connected to the adults who care for them, they derive their sense of well-being and self-worth from growing, caring, helping and sharing with and for other people. They develop an intrinsic locus of power and they're far less likely to be burdened by stress and anxiety.

So obsessed are we with seeking quick fixes that every magazine at the local grocery store has headlines such as "5 Tips for a Stress-free Life," "Axe Out Your Child's Anxiety for Good" and "3-Step Parenting." But as the philosopher Jiddu Krishnamurti once said, "Action has meaning only in relationship." Without the foundation of deep connection and emotional soothing, there is no room for teaching. By cultivating our own ability to learn through our children and better interpret their signals, we can create the circumstances that will naturally support their growth.

With support from an emotionally present and responsive adult, children can learn to harness stress and to tame and master it rather than avoid it. By facing challenges and reaching their limits of stress and anxiety without going past that point, children increase their resilience, self-esteem and feelings of capability. Our first step in leading the way towards openness, connection and joy is to understand the many facets of the problem itself.

TWO

WHAT EXACTLY IS ANXIETY?

To understand what anxiety is and isn't, we must first look at its close cousin, stress. Acute stress is short-lived and it is one of the greatest survival tools humans have. It focuses our attention to help us perform better in high-stakes situations; for example, it compels us to jump out of the way when a car veers in our direction or back off when a dog starts to growl at us. When we experience acute stress, different parts of the brain work hand in hand to assess the degree of danger we face and the amount of effort that is required to escape it. Then, a subconscious decision-making process automatically kicks into gear.

To understand what this means, it helps to know a bit about our *neurological system*. This is our information collection, processing and communication system, and it is made up of our *central nervous system* (the brain and the spinal cord) and our *peripheral nervous system* (the nerves that come from the brain and the spinal cord and that radiate to all our major organs). The *neural circuits* are all the pathways that send and receive messages throughout the body.

When dealing with stress, if we instinctively believe the danger is manageable, our fight-or-flight response is activated. In other words, the nervous system triggers a surge in the stress hormones epinephrine (adrenaline) and cortisol from the adrenal glands (near our kidneys) that put us on high alert. When children are scared, they might lash out in anger or run to their room because their heart is racing and their body is ready for action.

However, if we interpret the threat to be insurmountable, the brain tells our nervous system to freeze, or do the "dorsal dive." Our vagus nerve, which is located in the brain and is one of the largest nerves in the body, is responsible for regulating our heart rate, among other tasks. When we become anxious and our body becomes too aroused, the vagus nerve shuts down, causing a sudden drop in our blood pressure and our heart rate that sends us into physical and emotional collapse. This is one of our earliest evolutionary defense responses, and it's meant to trick predators into thinking we're no longer live prey so they lose interest and leave. Children who believe they're utterly helpless may feel their only recourse is to hold still and clam up, or in extreme cases, to collapse limply to the ground. If you've witnessed children in this state, you'll recall how difficult it is to console or reason with them.

There's a big difference, though, between the adaptive advantages of acute stress and the damaging effects of the chronic stress we—adults and children alike—face in our fast-paced, competitive modern world. A manageable degree of day-to-day stress is essential and even helpful, but too much stress interferes with the balance within the body.

Identifying anxiety

Anxiety and stress share similar symptoms, and even experts struggle to define the line between them. The hallmark of anxiety is longstanding, unbearable discomfort. With stress, the symptoms will dissipate once the stressor is removed, whereas in the case of anxiety, those symptoms of stress will continue whether the stressor is present or not. So how can parents recognize when normal levels of stress have mushroomed into anxiety? The answer lies in the persistence and severity of the discomfort.

Fact: People of all ages suffer from anxiety disorders and their symptoms are very similar, but they describe those symptoms differently depending on their age.

Look for symptoms that interfere with a child's ability to cope with the normal day-to-day demands of life, including physical, cognitive and emotional reactions. Think of it this way: many children have a healthy stress response to needles; after all, they hurt and they look scary. In fact, no rational being—child or adult—is soothed by the thought of them, and many people are afraid when they see a needle at the doctor's office. But when the stress of confronting needles becomes an obsessive fear that a child cannot let go of even when there are no needles in sight, what should be a natural and reasonable response becomes a serious problem of anxiety.

Myths and misunderstandings

A number of myths about anxiety and how it manifests in children continue to flourish, despite a cascade of studies debunking them. These common misunderstandings can make it hard to know what you're dealing with, let alone how to help—and they leave many anxious children unidentified or improperly diagnosed and without the support they so badly need.

MYTH 1: ANXIETY IS JUST ANOTHER NAME FOR FEAR.

Learning to face our fears is an important part of growth and development. Wrestling with the fear of separating from parents or starting a new school allows children to develop coping mechanisms, become resilient and resourceful and prepare for more serious life obstacles ahead.

If I asked you to picture an anxious child, you'd probably imagine a child struck by fear—a five-year-old on the first day of school, a ten-year-old on opening night of the school play or a twelve-year-old in the nurse's office on immunization day. But fear and anxiety are not one and the same. While they often go hand in hand, the neurobiology is different. As with stress, fear is a short-lived response to a specific trigger, whereas anxiety affects children in most areas of their lives and can manifest in ways that look nothing like fear.

Fact: Children worry most *frequently* about school, health and personal harm. They worry most *intensely* about family, friends and natural disasters.

Stella

Stella created an impression that remains vivid in my mind, years after our time together. Her brother, Daniel, was brought to me for treatment—he had autism and struggled to decipher the complex social cues so necessary in friendship. Isolated from his peers, he relied heavily on his eleven-year-old sister; in the playground, you could always find Stella by his side.

It was only by happenstance that Daniel's mother mentioned that Stella was struggling too, with mystery stomachaches her pediatrician couldn't solve, problems focusing at school and a nightly battle with falling asleep. I asked to spend a little time with Stella to find out more because I suspected there might be a connection between the stress of managing her brother's challenges and the civil war inside her body. In the play therapy room, Stella had an outpouring of emotion, first through art and stories, then through direct reflections on her life. She was compassionate and insightful beyond her years but carried a weight of responsibility that was heavier than she could bear.

Stella vacillated between holding her grief close like a protective shield and releasing the internalized fear and sense of responsibility that came with having a brother with a serious disability. Through therapy, she found the courage to ask for help. She implored her parents to talk with the school about playground bullying and the lack of adult support for her brother. Once they became more aware of the pressure she had been bearing, her parents arranged for a teacher's aide to work with Daniel on his friendship-building skills and set expectations for inclusion among his peers. They even helped create a Friends of Autism support group to help all the students better understand autism. In time, Stella's stomachaches and sleep troubles began to dissipate, as adults freed her from her sense of responsibility for Daniel's care and from the emotional pain of watching peers pick on her brother.

PARENTING STRATEGY: Children like Stella may not appear anxious. Far from fearful, they embody resilience and strength, and it's only when their body cries out that the hidden cost of stress and anxiety becomes apparent. Being aware that anxiety can take many forms and being curious about the root causes of our children's stress can help us to better identify unspoken thoughts, feelings and coping mechanisms that might be hurting rather than helping. When we are able to help our kids articulate their distress, we can more easily help them to confront and subdue the reasons behind it.

MYTH 2: PEOPLE WITH ANXIETY AREN'T TRYING HARD ENOUGH. KIDS SHOULD JUST SNAP OUT OF IT.

The assumption that anxiety is a motivational issue fuels the myth that eliminating it is simply a case of mind over matter. You'd be surprised how often parents assume that anxiety can be fixed through good old-fashioned hard work—after all, anxious kids should just snap out of it, try harder and change their attitude, right? Trust me when I tell you that no amount of blood, sweat and tears can pull children from the grip of anxiety solely through their own efforts.

Jessica

Several years ago, ten-year-old Jessica was referred to me by her school counselor, who was terribly concerned about the girl's test-related anxiety and increasing panic attacks. Jessica's father was convinced that she wasn't studying hard enough: if she tried harder, she would be better prepared and her problem would simply go away. He failed to see that Jessica was already putting herself under enormous pressure to be perfect and to please him and that his attitude only made her anxiety worse.

As Jessica mastered some breathing techniques, learned how to change her self-talk and faced her fear step-by-step, her panic attacks subsided. When I spoke with her father, he shared his own experience of growing up with parents who loved him but were distant and had high expectations he could never seem to meet. In time, he better understood his daughter's need for patience and compassion—and saw that Jessica's panic attacks could not have been wrestled into submission through willpower alone.

PARENTING STRATEGY: Keep in mind that avoidance behavior may be a symptom rather than a cause of anxiety—the child who panics at writing a test and fails or the child who doesn't prepare for a school performance is often anxious for reasons that have nothing to do with the test itself. Once we take the pressure off ourselves and our kids, we have more freedom to listen and identify what they're really thinking and feeling.

I've seen countless children forced to face challenges that far exceeded what their anxiety levels would permit them to do. As with Jessica, their parents were well meaning but took a misguided approach that backfired. Not only were those children left feeling that they had failed in their goal, they also carried a new sense of shame, believing that they'd let their parents down or didn't try hard enough. Knowing when to nudge our children forward and when to hold back is difficult. Often, we erroneously believe that anxious children can overcome their barriers if they work harder and if we push them—for their own good.

MYTH 3: ANXIETY IS A BEHAVIOR PROBLEM. PARENTS JUST NEED TO BE FIRMER.

Children who lash out with explosive tantrums or other forms of acting out are often assumed to be badly behaved or in need of firmer parenting. Too often we miss that they've become overwhelmed and can't find the words to describe what's happening inside. An anxious child who becomes irritable, angry or controlling is grasping at emotional straws, trying to say "there's something terribly wrong and I desperately need your help."

Jana

Jana's parents were concerned about her recent angry outbursts. When Jana first started to act out almost every day after returning from school, her parents had assumed she was just going through an adjustment phase, much like her older brother had done when he'd started first grade. Only in this case, showing empathy and setting firm limits made no difference. Instead, Jana's acting out continued to escalate beyond her parents' ability to soothe her or contain her temper.

The way her mother described Jana's behavior was completely contrary to what I witnessed. In my office, Jana never talked much, but when she did she was sweet and engaging. When she did reveal a little more about herself, she spoke strongly—mostly about her teacher, how *mean* she was and how all the children were scared of her. Jana's conviction told me there was truth behind her words, and her fits of rage at the end of the school day only corroborated the stories she told me.

After speaking with Jana, her parents and her teacher, it became clear that Jana was unaccustomed to being in an environment that emphasized structured lessons and strict rules rather than the creative play and relationship-building she was used to. In truth, the teacher didn't seem to delight in Jana's presence or understand her temperament. Without a trusted adult nearby, her fight-or-flight response was in overdrive and she was behaving in ways her parents had never seen in her before.

Once they were attuned to the fact that Jana's acting out was a call for help, her parents bolstered her with support and they made it through a tough school year together. When she was frustrated, Jana learned to voice the things she feared most about going to school rather than keeping them in and letting them overwhelm her. Jana's teacher never really adapted her approach, but it was enough for Jana that with her family being more aware of the situation, home was once more an emotionally safe place.

Jana visited me again the following year and shared in great detail the gift of having an *amazing* second-grade teacher. She was transformed, and her tantrums were long gone.

PARENTING STRATEGY: When children can't find the words to convey what's going on inside, it makes it difficult for adults to understand how they are really feeling. But we also need to remember that emotion and behavior are not separate. If, when we see children angry or acting out, we ask, "What's really causing this?" we will have taken a critical step towards understanding and compassion.

MYTH 4: ANXIETY IS A CHARACTER FLAW. SOME CHILDREN ARE JUST WIRED THIS WAY.

The idea that anxiety is a character weakness is by far one of the most destructive beliefs because it creates a stigma that is completely unfounded. The truth is that children with high anxiety may be every bit as strong as other children; the difference is that they're battling worries and fears other children just don't face in the same way. And in most cases, once they learn ways to defuse their irrational thoughts, their strength of character and spirit shines through. In fact, children with high anxiety are often more insightful, more perceptive and more sensitive than their peers. It's as if they are more acutely aware of details that others don't see or understand. When we are unable to see or relate to the cause of the anxiety, many of us become uncomfortable (as we are with any other mental health concern) and are left grappling for answers. Even if a child's high anxiety doesn't meet the criteria for a named disorder, the fear and lack of understanding around it leave many parents silenced. For their kids, the implications can be devastating.

Bryan

One of my first clients, twelve-year-old Bryan, was convinced that his debilitating fear of speaking in front of others was somehow his fault. Not only did he think he simply wasn't smart enough, he was sure that his anxiety was a punishment for being a bad person. He'd been paralyzed by fear for years, and when he could find no outside rationale he looked for an internal cause.

Through therapy, Bryan learned about the role his family's genetic history played in his anxiety, and how his brain and body perpetuated the feelings he worked so hard to avoid. He came to accept that his anxiety is in part hereditary and that he'd done nothing to bring it upon himself. It also became clear that he'd never hold at fault a friend who felt anxious or view them as *bad,* so he realized he didn't need to treat himself that way either. He was able to see anxiety as an experience, not an essential part of who he is.

> **PARENTING STRATEGY:** The good news here is that whether a child has serious clinical levels of anxiety or anxiety of a lesser degree, there are plenty of ways to curtail self-blame. By reassuring our children that anxiety is something we all experience, teaching them where it comes from and empowering them with tools to quell it, we send an invaluable message that anxiety can subside and that it is not their fault. Addressing stigma with education and showing compassion when we don't understand others can go far as we work towards solving the problem. Acknowledging that it can be as frustrating for those who are not being understood as it is for those who don't understand is a starting point for the kind of insight and change we're all looking for.

THREE

HOW ANXIETY AFFECTS DEVELOPMENT

Marta

Fourteen-year-old Marta would never have come for therapy had her father not taken away every book, TV remote, iPod and computer in the house. Suffering from agoraphobia, she had refused to attend her entire eighth grade year. Not only was Marta losing out on critical learning, she was losing out on the happiness that comes with being connected to others. Tears eventually came as she spoke of her loneliness. "I just want the same things other kids have: to go to parties and get into trouble and have memories with friends. It's not fair that my sister has all that and I'm the one who suffers."

It wasn't hard to feel for Marta. She'd had a panic attack that was followed by episodes of crying and, later, by stomachaches. Very quickly, she'd developed a fear of appearing in public. Although she'd seen a pediatrician, a psychiatrist, a community mental health team and numerous private therapists, these assessments had been largely unsuccessful in addressing the source of her anxiety. It wasn't yet clear whether my work with her would be any different.

As Marta returned week after week, she reluctantly spoke about her childhood years, her parents' divorce, her mother's struggle with breast cancer and her eventual death. While Marta's pain was palpable, she claimed, "None of that had anything to do with my anxiety. I don't remember being sad about it at all." What Marta didn't realize is that her feelings had been "bottled up" for so long that her body had been unable to process the trauma. This internal stress had disarmed her natural healing response and left her frozen—just as if she were facing a constant, unmanageable source of acute stress. In an attempt to protect itself, her brain was sending the message to disassociate from herself and all those who loved her. Eventually, this emotional lockdown, which accompanies trauma, became normal.

In Marta's case, the relationship between anxiety and her capacity to learn was complex and interrelated. School had once been a place of refuge for Marta, but the transition to a larger, more chaotic high school environment became too much for her to cope with. There, she had struggled with inattention, poor short-term memory and disorganization—all of which are common experiences of children with anxiety.

Anxiety affects school, school affects anxiety

Anxiety cripples our capacity to learn and disrupts the natural curiosity that is so imperative for children trying to manage in any school environment. Children in a constant state of stress and anxiety just can't think straight; chaotic heart and brain patterns interfere with the ability to process information. Imagine how frightening it must be to sit down to take a test and find yourself literally blanking out, unable to remember a math procedure or the spelling of certain words. "It makes sense at home, but when I go to write the test my mind just freezes," is a common complaint of students with anxiety. Brain science tells us one of the reasons why—chronically high cortisol levels released during stress can destroy brain cells in the hippocampus, the area of the brain responsible for forming long-term memories.

Children who are perfectionists tend to overproduce the dopamine necessary for sharp thinking and focused behavior, which puts their brains on a hyper-vigilant lookout for danger. In contrast, children who underproduce dopamine as a result of stress have more trouble focusing and thinking clearly, which leads to inattention, fatigue and a lack of motivation. Both too much and too little dopamine greatly reduce our ability to problem solve and learn.

Fact: In a 2012 nationwide study of nearly 4,000 teachers across Canada, 79% reported that helping students to cope with stress was a pressing concern in their classrooms, while 73% named anxiety disorders among their students as an increasingly important issue. Nearly 70% of public school teachers have not received professional development or training to address student mental illness in their classrooms.

In the classroom, teachers see anxiety-related distress show up as test anxiety, performance anxiety, non-compliance, behavior problems, withdrawal and social isolation. But rarely are they trained to identify and help manage their students' stress and anxiety. At conferences and training sessions, teachers frequently ask for practical solutions and tools they can implement easily as the demands of bigger and busier classrooms put pressure on both students and teachers.

In other cases, children with anxiety may seem to be managing well at school, and their teachers are often shocked to hear of a parent's concern. In fact, these children may be pulling it together during class time, but once they return to the safety of home, they drop their defense mechanisms and their internal distress shows up in dramatic ways. "My daughter comes home with a tummyache almost every day," parents tell me. "She's reactive and can't cope with homework. It takes me hours to settle her down at night." Meanwhile, the teacher is unresponsive to requests to pull back on homework or give extra time for projects. "They simply don't see or understand how distressed she is," say parents.

The opposite can also be true. Children who are stressed at school may appear relatively relaxed at home. Their fight-or-flight response kicks into high gear as they enter the perceived danger zone of the classroom. Parents of these children tell me, "I keep getting daily complaints from the school and requests that I have my son assessed, but at home he's perfectly happy." Subtler signs of anxiety can be overlooked; however, missing school because of stomachaches, headaches and other mystery ailments is an enormous red flag that something is wrong. Marta's father naturally wanted to soothe and protect his daughter from the distress of anxiety and trusted the problem would pass. He had no idea that allowing Marta to remain at home would so strongly reinforce the idea that school was a scary and dangerous place—or that it would lead from days and months to a whole year of avoiding school.

Fact: Children who are struggling with a problem are more likely to confide in a friend (50%) rather than a mother (30%), a father (10%) or a health care provider (22%).

When anxiety meets learning disabilities

While any child can develop anxiety, a study by Nelson and Harwood in the *Journal of Learning Disabilities* tells us the 6 percent of children and adolescents with learning disabilities face daily frustrations as they try to keep up with their peers, and the stress caused by standing out can naturally affect their anxiety levels. They're also particularly prone to social anxiety, which can make talking in class, fitting in with their peers and participating in groups a terrifying experience. It's like the whole world is judging their every move. And while anxiety can't *cause* a learning disability, it can affect a child's capacity to take in, process and remember information. In fact, children with learning disabilities are six times more likely to complain of fatigue, a common indication of anxiety.

When learning disabilities and anxiety appear together, it can be a slow process of trial and error to determine which is the primary concern; however, knowing which one to manage first can save much unnecessary struggle.

Long-term implications of unchecked anxiety

All stress is not created equal. While short-lived stress (such as attending a new school or trying a new sport) causes minor physiological changes like increased heart rate and changes in hormonal levels, it's long-term stress that leads to permanent changes in brain development. Almost every child is born with a healthy brain and vigor of spirit that thrives in the right conditions; however, stress and anxiety can crush that spirit and leave children vulnerable.

In his book *When the Body Says No,* author Dr. Gabor Maté talks in depth about his years as a medical coordinator of the Palliative Care Unit at Vancouver General Hospital, where he treated many patients with chronic illness. Their emotional histories were consistent: all had suffered unbearable levels of hidden stress. While persistent, untreated stress may not necessarily lead to radical problems like diabetes, multiple sclerosis or inflammatory bowel disease, it does diminish immune activity. In other words, high levels of stress hormones in the body can leave children vulnerable to infections and chronic health concerns.

Beyond the physical effects, there are other compelling reasons to take anxiety seriously. Low self-esteem, academic difficulties, behavioral issues and substance abuse are among the problems that anxious children are more likely to face. Self-medicating with drugs and alcohol is a common coping mechanism as children become teens; it is a maladaptive attempt to manage the symptoms of their anxiety. Depression, eating disorders and suicidal thoughts and attempts are all more likely among those with anxiety. According to both American and Canadian census reports, suicide is the second leading cause of death for youth, yet the societal trend is to ignore anxiety. Many parents hope that if they "wait it out," their child's anxiety will dissipate on its own. They too feel entrenched in deep discomfort wondering when or if it will pass. Ironically, this waiting and wondering reinforces powerlessness and further intensifies anxiety.

Much is still unknown about the full impact of stress and anxiety on the brain system, but what we do know is alarming. Prolonged exposure to high levels of stress can impair the neural circuitry, prevent developing brains from growing to full size and compromise the functioning of the hippocampus, which is responsible for learning and memory. These effects can last well into adulthood.

So often when I treat adults with anxiety I hear them say, "How might my life have been different if I'd known then what I know now?" And while we don't want to dwell on that question for too long, it is natural to wonder. Many adults are only now coming across concepts such as mindfulness, mood and thought regulation, relaxation and turning inward. It's worth turning the question around: "How might the world be different for our children if we make connection and mindfulness (and all the tools that come with them) part of our day-to-day life?"

FOUR

ANXIETY AND THE FAMILY

It's no secret that our thoughts and feelings are affected by those around us, and a crying baby, an angry spouse or an anxious child can all trigger an emotional response. We're hardwired to tune in to signals from those around us and pay attention to the needs of others, and the roots of this function run deeper than you might think.

If you've ever felt "infected" by another person's bad mood or "swept up" in someone else's attitude, you know that our ability to affect each other goes beyond the thoughts and feelings we might have about each other's actions. If it sometimes feels as if your closest friends and family members get right inside your head, you're exactly right. And when parenting thought leader Peggy O'Mara said, "The way we talk to our children becomes their inner voice," she was right. The science of interpersonal neurobiology, which studies the ongoing interactions between the mind, the brain and relationships by drawing on and integrating research from many different disciplines, tells us that when we interact with others, our eyes and ears are taking in verbal and nonverbal information about each other while our brains are busy having a conversation all their own.

The exchange of information that allows us to relate to others emotionally is called interpersonal integration, and it's an essential social function. Our brains contain cells called neurons that transmit messages to the body. Among these are "mirror neurons," which compel us to echo the intentions of the people we are connected to. At the simplest level, mirror neurons cause us to yawn when others yawn, and at the most complex level they are responsible for the attachment of parent to child. It's the mirror response that affects us so deeply when our children are acting out their anxiety. Not only are we upset to see them in distress; our brains are actually working to mirror theirs, making it harder for us to access a place of calm in ourselves. We literally match each other's emotional states.

Every time a child laughs, cries, hugs, throws a tantrum or lashes out, the brain of every family member is altered. And the responses will depend upon each person's temperament, level of development, coping style and relationship with the child. When responding to a child with anxiety, some people may become impatient or frustrated whereas others will attempt to solve the problem for the child or distance the child from stressors. These varied responses reflect different ways to cope with empathy and the discomfort it stirs up. Of course, a child's brain system is also affected by the emotional state of those around them, which means that family members can consciously help to create a supportive and empathetic dynamic. Achieving this is easier said than done. However, it may help to know there's a very real and scientific basis for that lingering upset we feel when our children are in distress. From that understanding, we can move towards intentionally fostering connected and balanced relationships within the whole family.

Understanding sibling reactions

How children react to having a sibling with anxiety varies depending on their age and level of development. And feelings aren't static; in fact, how siblings feel about each other can be something of a moving target.

Younger children find it more difficult to understand the situation and interpret events concretely. At times, young kids resent the attention their parents give to the anxious sibling because they see it as a threat to their own parent-child attachment. And, if no one talks about the anxiety, children are left with a deep sense that something is wrong but they can't say what. It's difficult enough for adults to know how to cope with a child's anxiety, but imagine how distressing it must be for a sibling. As a four-year-old, it's hard to explain to your mom or dad that it upsets you to see your sibling screaming in terror at the sight of a bee or sobbing at the thought of going to school, or to see your parents angry that your brother or sister is asking to sleep in their bed yet again. Internalizing all these thoughts and feelings can be distressing and disrupt our children's well-being.

Ava

Six-year-old Ava was brought to see me because she was becoming angry and defiant, seemingly out of the blue. As I spoke with her about her older sister, Madison, I learned that she had become frustrated because Madison's anxiety was causing her to be terribly unkind, fracturing their sibling bond.

AVA: "Madison is always mean. She bosses me and wouldn't let me play when my cousins came over."

ME: "It must feel unfair when she's not nice to you. What did you do when she wouldn't let you play?"

AVA: "I ripped up the picture she was doing, and my mom made me go to my room."

ME: "You were so mad you ripped up her picture, and then you got in trouble. Is there something that sometimes works better?"

AVA: "No. Madison *always* wants me to play with her, and when my cousins come over she's mean and won't let me play. And my mom and dad don't listen."

Ava's parents were working hard to address Madison's anxiety, and having her cousins over to play seemed a great way to compensate for the social problems she faced at school. But Madison resented Ava's ease in social situations and wanted to control playtime for herself. In our sessions, I learned that Ava was being shamed, ridiculed, ignored and excluded by her sister. While Ava's parents were trying to protect Madison, they'd inadvertently triggered Ava's worst fear—that she was being abandoned. Being shut out by Madison and then sent to her room by her parents at a time when she most needed soothing and guidance only exacerbated Ava's natural competitiveness with her sister; in her mind, Madison's needs were more important than her own. Her insecurity and frustration naturally led to aggression, and the pain of separation made her more hostile, not less.

As Ava was encouraged not to "rock the already unsteady boat," she was learning to deny her deeper feelings of fear, anger and embarrassment that she had to look out for her much bigger sister. When I asked Ava about her feelings she often answered *we* rather than *me;* her concern about Madison was causing her to lose her sense of self. Remaining constantly tuned in to another human being requires a lot of mental energy and attention, and children who are required to do it become less tuned in to themselves in order to accomplish the task.

KIDS IN PRIMARY school are more socially minded than older children and tend to feel embarrassed or ashamed about differences between their anxious sibling and someone else's brother or sister. They may worry about "catching" the problem and they may feel guilty because their sibling is suffering while they are not (at least not to the same degree). While some kids will protect or guide their sibling through the anxiety, others will push them away to try to separate themselves from the discomfort. Teens too can disengage

Fact: Nearly 60% of all children worry a lot or all the time about the health of someone they love.

but they are more likely to "parent" an anxious sibling, regardless of the age gap. They may feel frustrated that their mom or dad hasn't been able to fix the problem, so they step in to soothe their own distress. Looking after their sibling doesn't help with their own anxiety, though, and their need to control can come across as bossy and controlling, making things worse for everyone concerned.

In essence, one child's anxiety can activate their siblings' own fear response, absorb their parents' attention and even derail family plans. Imagine the frustration of missing a concert, family dinner or shopping trip because your brother or sister is having a panic attack and can't seem to make it out the door, or the powerlessness of witnessing it and not being able to help. While the effects of anxiety on siblings are unquestionably real, there are many ways parents can help to alleviate the discomfort. In chapter 5, you'll find guidance on how to talk about the problem with respect and responsibility, and it's a conversation to have with siblings too. And as you incorporate the tools from chapter 6 into your life, you will open the door for everyone in the family to voice their concerns and maintain a healthy sense of self.

Parenting children with anxiety

One of the biggest fears of any parent whose child is suffering from anxiety is: did I somehow cause this? It's terrible to think that we might somehow have contributed to our children's distress. As soothing as it would be to say otherwise, it has to be acknowledged that as parents we do play a part, both genetically and behaviorally. Our influence begins at conception. The genetic links are undeniable, and if anxiety runs in your family history, you can assume your children are coming by their own anxiety honestly, at least from a biological standpoint. So how does nurture come into play?

One of our highest goals as parents is to help our children find emotional equilibrium. These are the times when the flow and connection with our children is seamless and in tune; it literally feels magical. When our children are happy and engaged and there's an ease in the relationship, we know their attachment is secure. It's as though there exists a spirit-to-spirit connection. Our ability to reach that goal largely depends upon our ability to take care of our own well-being, which can seem impossible when we see our children struggling.

Difficult times can throw everything out of sync, including parenting. When we're disconnected or emotionally off balance, our children's natural response is to disengage, and before long the dynamic between parent and child is in a downward spiral. We are no longer conscious of the full range of our thoughts and feelings or the needs of our child. When anxiety hits, we often become either more controlling or we retreat. Both responses can increase our children's distress. In these moments, we can find ourselves becoming inflexible and unwilling to compromise. I call this "stuck-in-the-mud parenting" because no one is going anywhere. In this mode, our hyperrational left-brain thinking is attempting to regain a sense of control (albeit unsuccessfully) and we have little ability to empathize and connect with others. At other times, our emotional right-brain thinking takes over and we become purely reactive. I can best describe this as "parenting without a parachute" because our ability to reason and use logic is lost in the cosmos and we're in free fall, with no equipment to help navigate safely through the winds of emotion. In this mode, we're inadvertently exacerbating our children's anxiety levels by modeling fear, anxious behavior and fragile coping skills.

It's natural to lose our cool once in awhile, and it can actually be helpful for children to see we have our emotional limits. But going into free fall on a regular basis interferes with our deepest parenting intention, which is to foster well-attached, emotionally trusting children. By keeping our own anxiety in check and putting the health of our family and connection above all else, we can directly counteract the emotional free floating that is so pervasive in our children. After all, we cannot give to others what we cannot give to ourselves.

When we're in a state of equilibrium, we have access to emotional information as well as to logic. We're calm, aware, empathetic, and at the same time we're helping our children to understand the situation and find solutions. These are the moments that feel like hitting a parenting home run as our children's tension melts away in our care. By practicing self-care and conscientiously clearing away as much of our own emotional interference as is realistically possible, we're protecting our parenting purpose and living the message that children and parents matter to each other. In turn, through attachment and loving guidance we can win back our children from stress and anxiety as they learn to trust the world around them.

CALMING OUR OWN EMOTIONAL WATERS

The apple really doesn't fall far from the tree: none of us likes to admit it, but anxious parents make for anxious kids. When parents wrestle with heightened anxiety, their children are at a double risk of developing anxiety by inheriting it and by seeing it modeled. Running late, forgetting commitments, having difficulty sleeping, becoming irritable and scrambling from one responsibility to the next are all markers that anxiety is interfering with our ability to be consciously aware, and this can trigger anxiety in our children too.

While the genes we inherit largely determine the degree of anxiety we're faced with, our temperament, innate coping abilities and outside stressors all add to the mix. Separating our own anxiety from our children's isn't easy. By paying close attention to our thoughts, emotions and even sensations in the body, we can tune in to our "core self" to find clarity, insight and even joy in the midst of what may feel like a parenting crisis.

Kendra

"I have no idea what to do anymore," Kendra told me when we first met. "I'm exhausted and I know I'm doing a terrible job. The other day Lucas didn't want to leave the park, and after all kinds of warnings I finally just walked away. I knew he wouldn't stay behind, and I felt terrible because he was so panicked that I'd just leave him. He followed me, crying and screaming. It was heartbreaking, but I was at my limit."

"You must have been terribly frustrated," I said. "Let's talk this through and find out together what's lighting up within you. From there, it may be easier to find what Lucas needs in those difficult moments."

Kendra explained, "With most kids you'd just tell them, 'It's time to go. I'm starting the walk home' and they'd switch gears knowing you meant business. But Lucas gets so stressed that I don't have that option. When we got home, it was a full evening of 'You don't love me. You just left me at the park and didn't care.' The last thing he needs is to feel abandoned, so there are days when I end up giving in to whatever he wants and I know that isn't helping."

"When Lucas moves into that emotional and behavioral storm, it's scary and painful for you—and at times you feel you've lost your parenting compass."

"I'm trying so hard to stay consistent, but his negativity wears me down. I sometimes wonder if I'm the right mother for him. I have so much anxiety myself, I don't know where his anxiety stops and mine begins. It's like our whole household is in distress and I'm failing my family."

Kendra is so generous of heart that I couldn't help but want to reassure her of her strength and capability. But I knew all the reassurance in the world wouldn't soothe her for long. She was carrying unbearable burdens of loss and a lifetime of attempts to be everything to everyone.

Kendra's recounting of her life history explained a great deal. Her own mother was unpredictable, angered easily and berated her father over seemingly minor things. Kendra had recently picked up *Stop Walking on Eggshells* by Paul Mason, a book written for those trying to survive life with a loved one with borderline personality disorder, and she was astonished by the similarities between composites in the book and her own experience.

Kendra's dad had died from heart failure three years earlier. He had been a great support, and without his stable love and attachment it's unlikely she would have survived her childhood with the same degree of strength and tenacity. He'd been a safe haven for her. When her mother had collapsed in fits of tears and rage or withdrew for days complaining of migraines or endometriosis, he'd taken Kendra to work with him. It was a diversion Kendra came to rely on, but her mother resented this bond between Kendra and her father. It fed her paranoia and only further reinforced her tendency to see Kendra as conniving, selfish and playing on her father's emotional side. Although there were moments when she'd appear charming and fun, these never lasted.

Most parents struggle to find a healthy balance between their child's needs and their own, but Kendra's needs rarely came first. Even as an adult, she had trouble asserting herself, and her own children felt her sense of powerlessness every time she set a boundary but backed down if anyone challenged her. Without consistency, her kids grew more anxious because it's hard to feel safe in the world when your parent is unable to set and hold boundaries that might protect you from harm.

Remembering her mother's erratic parenting style was affecting Kendra's reactions and emotions, and her son was picking up on her feelings of self-blame, dread and panic. Her fear of the powerful emotional reactions of others was leading her to overreact, which essentially reinforced her son's belief that emotion is scary. As Kendra worked hard to understand and accept her own history, retelling it in parent-focused therapy, she learned to focus on her resilience and use coping tools to more confidently manage the distress in her children. By bringing the past into her present and reprocessing old reactions, she better understood where she stopped and her child began, which allowed her to set and maintain clear boundaries. And in quieting her own mind, Kendra was better able to hear her children's fear and respond with more compassion in those difficult parenting moments.

AS YOU MOVE through this book, I encourage you to look at the impact of your own past. Doing this work serves our own healing and growth, leaving more emotional room to help our children begin to understand themselves and cultivate a value system that reflects their beliefs. It frees us up to model mindful awareness, to be present and responsible for our emotions and reactions, and to demonstrate positive, balanced coping strategies for our children. It's an approach that draws us closer to ourselves and closer to our children.

Recognizing parental coping styles

When our own anxiety causes us to lose our connection with our higher parenting purpose we become focused on our own ego-driven needs, and it can change our parenting styles more than we may realize.

Study upon study shows us anxiety can increase our tendency to use a "corporal parenting style." We can become more intrusive, forceful and controlling with our kids—and that can cause our children to become more inhibited and withdraw from our care. The extreme end of corporal parenting is spanking, which is usually a panic reaction when we feel we've lost our power. Any physical discipline undermines our children's trust and ruptures their ability to turn to us for guidance; instead they recoil or scramble to reconnect with us emotionally. It can't be said strongly enough that spanking will not create the positive changes or mutually respectful relationship we're looking for. Its impact tends to be a predictable pattern of increasing anxiety throughout childhood.

An overly controlling or forceful parenting style isn't the only one that causes children stress. As we'll see, overprotective and permissive parenting styles are a problem too. Children and youth raised by adults with these parenting styles tend to disconnect from their emotions because they are either unable to voice their needs or strongly discouraged or dismissed when they do.

You will probably notice yourself using each of these coping styles from time to time as you try a variety of different lines of attack—no parent fits into only one category. Please don't be too hard on yourself or take this as judgment; thousands of parents are wrestling with similar concerns (myself included) and it's their reported experiences that have led to these descriptions. Naming them is meant to help identify culturally based parenting trends that simply aren't working, not add to the parenting shame minefield. When we examine our own patterns, we are better able to objectively consider the benefits and drawbacks of our approach and work to restore our connection with our anxious kids by showing empathy and compassion.

THE CORPORAL

Parents who believe the tough-love approach is the right way to go tend to see anxiety as a weakness and struggle with their own feelings of vulnerability. They believe that children who grow a thick skin are stronger and more resilient to life's pitfalls. While corporals may initially try to be positive in the face of their children's anxiety, frustration and anger and a fear that their kids are missing out on key life events can cause them to respond harshly. As they scramble to banish their children's distress, their forceful approach backfires as it adds to the distance between them.

Fact: More than one-third of children report experiencing headaches in any given month, but only rarely do parents consider these to be the result of stress.

If this sounds familiar, your own internal distress may be affecting your brain system in complex ways. The left side of the brain, which is responsible for language, logic and linear thinking, likes order and predictability. In contrast, the right side of the brain, which is responsible for emotion and intuition, looks at the overall meaning of an experience. In corporals, the left-brain may have plenty of logical ideas for eliminating stress and anxiety; however, these may be overriding the capacity of the right-brain to provide the soothing that's so essential before our children will listen to what we're offering. In other words, the left-brain "letter of the law" is overriding the right-brain "spirit of the law."

When corporals believe that their children aren't trying hard enough, these parents tend to lose patience and react in ways that leave them feeling guilty. They may think, "If my kids would just follow what I'm asking them to do, they'd be fine." Corporals may also struggle to distinguish between *who their child is* and *what their child does* and they may not always be conscious of how scary their frustration can be for their children. There's a big difference between "You hit your brother" and "You're a bad person." Caught in a vicious circle of stepping in quickly because it's so hard to see kids struggle and learn for themselves, corporals end up with children whose fear (and shame) becomes entrenched.

> **PARENTING STRATEGY:** If this is you, imagine what might be possible if you learn to calm your own internal waters and restrain your impulse to forcefully jump in, but still remain present and available. Picture your children naturally leaning into you, gradually becoming more emotionally self-reliant and processing their own anxiety rather than avoiding it.

THE OVERPROTECTOR

Parents who feel like they're walking on thin ice constantly monitor their children for signs that they're getting treacherously close to their stress threshold. Overprotectors carefully try to avoid saying the *wrong thing* and will do whatever it takes to prevent their children from facing anxiety. These parents are often anxious themselves and work extremely hard to prevent problems and act as a buffer between their children and the world.

Overprotectors tend to constantly comfort their kids by telling them that "Things will be okay" or "It's really not that bad" and are often trying to "move them along emotionally." They are well intentioned but often uncomfortable with their children's anxiety and powerful feelings, so they use general statements as a short-term solution. Without taking the time to fully acknowledge how hard things are, listen to their kids and challenge them, overly protective parents can leave their children feeling disconnected, invalidated and unable to develop their own solutions.

It is completely natural for parents to want to step in whenever kids are struggling, especially parents of children with anxiety whose urge to rescue their child from distress is incredibly overwhelming. After all, is that not our job as parents? The danger is that in this state, overprotectors may be dangerously close to "parenting without a parachute." They may be feeling their children's anxiety to such an extreme degree that they become emotionally chaotic themselves and look for short-term solutions such as accommodating their kids' fears by vigilantly trying to anticipate and avoid the emotional triggers and by failing to place boundaries on the behaviors associated with those fears. Kids of overprotectors find it harder to take the risks necessary to face fears and test out their skills and internal resources. Like all children, they take their cues from their parents; in this case, those messages falsely tell them that the world is a dangerous place.

> **PARENTING STRATEGY:** If this is you, consider some of the early messages you may have internalized about negative emotion. Imagine how your life may have been different if you were taught that "There is no bad emotion, and both pleasant and unpleasant feelings are equally important." Instead, close your eyes, take your own mindful moment and accept the sensations and emotions that arise. Simply watch them ebb and flow, welcoming whatever happens to show up. And keep in mind, no emotion lasts forever, whether that's your child's or your own.

THE PERMISSIVE PARENT

Permissive parents are super easygoing. They believe the best way to manage children's anxiety is to avoid stress, disagreements and conflict of any kind. Like all parents, they tire of the behavioral implications of their children's anxiety and adapt by loosening their parenting boundaries. The lack of parenting guidance that permissiveness creates, fractures the parent-child attachment and holds kids back from developing the self-confidence that naturally unfolds in the hierarchy of the parent-child relationship.

Unfortunately, the lack of consistent firm and loving limits so necessary for children to feel safe in the world exacerbates the anxiety of children parented by permissive parents. The lack of proactive problem solving that goes hand in hand with this parenting style sends the implicit message that uncomfortable feelings should be avoided. And instead of facing the problem with strategies and understanding, the anxiety triggers become reinforced.

> **PARENTING STRATEGY:** If this is you, it may help to remind yourself that you are the most powerful tool your children have if they are to face their discomfort. By holding your boundaries, you will be teaching your children that there really is order and predictability in the world, and the structure you provide will help your kids internalize a sense of stability.

Learning to cope with wisdom

Whatever counterproductive patterns we may have fallen into, the remedy is the same: practice self-awareness, take a moment to find our own center, give our children permission to exist in whatever state they happen to be in (including anxiety) and help them to process whatever happens to be showing up emotionally. Doing these things sends the message: "I can handle anything you have to bring me."

A great side benefit of teaching our children to use the play-based tools in chapter 6 of this book is that we will master them ourselves along the way. Together, we will be deep-breathing our way out of sticky spots and thought-busting ourselves into a very different mindset. When we're not dealing with anxiety, we're more accepting and sensitive in our responses and our parenting is more integrated and balanced.

> ### Bringing the joy back into parenting
> Coming back to conscious awareness of our parenting purpose can bring us to a place that is higher than thoughts, emotions and actions. From there, joy naturally unfolds. Centering on the intention to learn through and with our children, mutually respect one another and delight in our shared existence can wash away power struggles and fear.

Working as a parenting team

Parenting together can be one of the brightest human joys, but it can also be one of our biggest sources of frustration, especially when our children are struggling. Even the most compatible couples have differing views on how best to parent their kids. We all want the support of a collaborative parenting partnership, but our ideal vision of what that looks like isn't always in alignment with our partner's. One large-scale American study by Stanley, Markman and Whitton published in the journal *Family Process* found that couples in their first marriage argue most about money, with children a close second. And in second marriages, children top the list of argument topics. Disagreement about bedtimes, chores, screen time, homework and parenting priorities are only a few of the areas that can trigger a heated discussion.

Different approaches aren't always a problem—children really do adapt to all kinds of parenting styles. For example, Dad is fussy about table manners; Mom is more relaxed. So when Dad's working late and Mom's in charge, the elbows spend a little more time on the table. It's really how parents resolve their differences that matters most, and whether they support each other on the bottom line. When parents respect one another's viewpoint, the whole family wins.

TIPS FOR POSITIVE CO-PARENTING

Expect conflict now and then. A clash in parenting styles is unavoidable from time to time and doesn't mean the relationship is in trouble. When you notice your emotions (or your partner's) rising, take a moment to determine where the issue fits into your parenting priorities before continuing. There's a wide divide between your ideal solution and the unacceptable, with a lot of room in between for compromise.

Aim for a speedy resolution. One of the best predictors of a happy family is swift conflict resolution, even if that means agreeing to disagree. Children (especially those with a sensitive temperament) are highly attuned to parent-to-parent interactions; their survival relies on it. When you resolve issues quickly without allowing your ego to get in the way, you teach your children the art of acceptance and compromise. This is a gift for any child, especially one already struggling with anxiety. If necessary, put a time limit on the discussion and agree to revisit it later to safeguard your children's sense of stability.

Help children make sense of your disagreement. I'm always amazed when I realize just how much my children are absorbing. Even wearing headphones and sitting in another room, they will readily pick up that "something's up," even from a whisper. While we all do our best to avoid arguing within earshot of our children, they inevitably notice our transgressions. Instead of ignoring the hot-button moment, use it as an opportunity to build understanding.

Children with anxiety often blame themselves for their parents' quarrels, especially when they are the subject of the conflict. Children need to know that disagreements are a normal part of any relationship and that, as long as there is mutual respect and healthy ground rules for communication, they don't have to be scary. It's reassuring for your kids to see that while you may not always like what someone says or does, you are always ready to make amends.

Give priority to family routine. Researchers at Syracuse University have confirmed something my grandmother has been saying for years: families that remain connected, thrive. After reviewing fifty years' worth of studies, Spagnola and Fiese reported in *Infants and Young Children* that when families eat breakfast and dinner together and maintain some kind of family routine, everyone gains. Children in these families are healthier overall, parents feel more satisfied with their marriage, and both parents and children are less stressed.

Whether you routinely cuddle up with your child to read at the end of the day or spend every Sunday hiking together, your special family activities provide more than fun—they provide security as everyone inherently senses the unity and connection deepening.

Move from auto-pilot to co-pilot. When children are struggling with anxiety, the burden of managing the problem usually falls on the shoulders of one parent in particular, which can naturally lead to resentment or feelings of alienation. When it comes to major parenting decisions, try to press the "pause" button before jumping in to just "take care of it" yourself. Instead, take a minute or two to sneak away to another room and have a quick conversation with your partner about how you'd like to address the tough issue together.

Present a united front. Children develop many strategies for getting what they want, including exploiting weak spots in their parents' relationship. Pitting one parent against another is a sign of their distress because it shows that they are no longer looking to us for answers but rejecting our guidance instead. When your children complain to you about your partner, use that opportunity to teach them how to address issues directly. Encourage them to share their frustration with the person they are angry with so they learn to take responsibility for their feelings rather than simply blowing off steam. When children see that their attempt to have you overrule your partner (or vice versa) isn't working, they experience firsthand that your family won't be divided and emotional integrity can be held intact.

Stay connected. According to relationship specialist and researcher John Gottman, almost 70 percent of couples describe feeling less satisfied with their marriage after having their first child. With the many demands of parenting leaving little time for intimacy, it can be difficult for parents to remain connected to themselves let alone to each other. And parents whose children are struggling with anxiety use a great deal of their energy tending to the parent-child attachment, which leaves even less available to partners who need that connection too. Committing to kid-free time together sends the message that you value your partnership and the foundation it provides for the whole family.

Look for new solutions. One of the most important things to remember when problem solving together is this: "the problem" isn't the real problem; the old solution is the problem. By looking at what hasn't worked, you can avoid making the same mistakes and finding yourselves in exactly the same position again and again. Instead, brainstorm together, talk to friends, take an attachment-focused parenting course or try couples' counseling. Do whatever it takes to keep the conversation open.

Nurturing partnership

The skills we develop as parents can also help us to resolve our issues as partners, as long as we hold ourselves to the same standards of mutual respect that we have set for our relationship with our children. By staying on target during discussions, getting over grudges, refusing to play the blame game and reaching out to reconnect, we can foster more resilient partnerships as well as happier children.

So often, we act in the same ways as the adults we witnessed in our own childhood, and these patterns can interfere with our ability to embody the qualities that healthy partnership requires. After all, it's hard to be mindful and emotionally open when alarm bells from our past are ringing loudly. As a reminder of the qualities you'd like to consciously bring to the conversation (and to yourself), think of the word "CLEAR," which means we connect *calmly*, *listen* actively with an *easy* manner, while being *attentive* and *responsive*.

These may seem to be simple suggestions, but we fall off this intent more often than we may realize.

Calm: Imagine how different life would be if you set an intention with your co-parent to talk about difficult topics only when you are both calm. While this notion might seem obvious (or maybe impossible), reminding yourselves of the emotional mindset you hope to set for yourselves really does help. I know many parents who have made a pact to remind each other of their intentions if ever their emotions run too high. For some couples, a nine out of ten is the stopping point; for others, it can be lower. Wherever your personal threshold lies, making an agreement to take a break if you or your partner is approaching the "red zone" is a wise and responsible thing to do.

Listen actively: Have you ever noticed all the wild and wooly ways you avoid hearing your partner instead of listening actively? You might be rehearsing your rebuttal, filtering the conversation to hear only what you want to, second guessing your partner's meaning, daydreaming (after all, do you really want to hear your partner tell you their take on the problem, yet again?), sparring with argumentative commentary, derailing the conversation by changing the subject, placating your partner by insincerely agreeing too quickly or advising by focusing on solutions.

As hard as it may be, resist the impulse to "jump in." Instead, try to repeat back to your partner what you heard. If ever you've been to couples' counseling, you'll recognize this as a tried-and-tested communication exercise. Many people resist this technique at first, as it can feel a little unnatural and goofy. But you'd be surprised by how often couples selectively hear or misread each other altogether. Checking what you've heard allows you to clarify the message and leaves your partner feeling authentically understood. That simple act alone can make difficult conversations feel safer emotionally.

Easy: Next, think about tapping into your easy vibe to open up communication. Take a deep breath, put up your clear fluid boundary (page 214) and do whatever it takes to maintain an approachable, relaxed attitude. Try bringing playfulness and humor to your conversations, even as you discuss challenges. Keep in mind, how the message is received has more to do with how we say it, than what is said. As adults, we often lose touch with our lighter side, trading it for a seriousness that weighs us down emotionally. Imagine what a difference it might make to bring delight to your discussion.

Attentive: Being attentive is more challenging now than ever before. The simple act of sitting down, relaxing your hands and engaging directly with your partner can be a tall order, as cell phones, computers and, of course, your kids compete for your attention. Picture what it would be like to focus entirely on what your partner is saying for the first few minutes of each and every conversation. Sound challenging? Well, it certainly is, but the mental discipline is one of the most beneficial choices you can make, and when you and your partner commit to being attentive to each other, you can trust that you'll get time to share your perspective too.

Responsive: Being responsive means tapping into high-order thinking, including empathy and selflessness. It entails not only intellectually understanding your partner's point of view but also acknowledging its value. When you can name the validity in your partner's perspective before you launch into your own, you create an opening for new ideas in your co-parenting and you nurture and deepen your relationship. Imagine the insights that can emerge! By tuning into your shared parenting attachment, you can avoid undermining each other and remain open to each other's insights about your child. You won't always agree, but even when you disagree you can always continue to honor your partner.

Parenting is not perpetually smooth sailing, but remember: no one knows our children better than we do, and no one is more motivated and better equipped to help them—even if we might doubt ourselves from time to time. I've met thousands of parents over the years. When I ask them what matters most about their parenting, I often hear different versions of the same thing: they want their child to thrive and they want to thrive themselves.

A family is more than the sum of its parts; it's an emotional and psychological ecosystem whose healthy functioning depends upon the harmony among its elements. Every family member has a profound effect on every other one, but as a parent you hold a special power to guide, nurture and direct the growth of your clan from your own self-awareness. It's my hope that through this work you'll find new resources to bring deeper connection, trust and psychological intimacy not only to your relationship with your child, but to your entire family.

FIVE

OVERCOMING CHILDHOOD ANXIETY WITH PLAY-BASED THERAPY

As parents, we naturally wish to set our children on a path of health and wellness so they can fully empower themselves and experience happiness and fulfillment in life. When anxiety threatens to disrupt their healthy development, we must seek out resources and treatment to restore their peace of mind and optimal functioning. This is more easily said than done. Anxiety is highly complex, and some types of clinical anxiety are harder to address than others. At times, we can become frustrated and even desperate when long-term solutions seem elusive.

Fortunately, the remedy for clinical levels of anxiety is clearer and more accessible than for some other serious childhood problems. Cognitive behavior therapy (CBT) is hands down the most well-supported approach to treatment and it has been clinically proven to offer lasting success. This evidence-based therapy deals with the interrelatedness of our thoughts, feelings and behavior, and it is built on the premise that by changing one, we can transform the other. Essentially, if we choose to *think* differently, in turn we'll *feel* and *behave* differently. And if we *behave* differently, we'll *think* and *feel* differently and so on. The result, when we consciously think and act in positive ways, is an integrated and sustainable improvement in our overall experience.

There's a well-accepted Buddhist quote that states, "Rule your mind or it will rule you." CBT teaches children to challenge anxious thoughts rather than accept them as truth. It arms them with a new mindset, tools to disrupt faulty thinking habits, and coping skills that cue the body's relaxation response. The core techniques of CBT work by helping children to

1. Understand that anxiety involves three things: thoughts (cognitions), behaviors and feelings (both emotional and physical).
2. Identify unhelpful and negative thought patterns and beliefs. These thoughts are called "thinking errors," but with kids I call them "thinking traps."
3. Replace these thinking traps with more helpful thoughts— essentially to change their mindset or inner dialogue.
4. Identify unhealthy behaviors that contribute to anxiety.
5. Replace unhealthy behaviors with self-supporting behaviors, such as deep breathing and progressive relaxation, and systematically confront the things that trigger their fear.

Backed by decades of scientific research, CBT is now widely considered the treatment of choice for anxiety and depression in both children and adults. Both the Canadian and US Psychological Association support CBT as the first course of remedial action—and for children at risk of anxiety or depression, it's the most effective method of prevention. CBT helps to limit the degree and persistence of anxiety and, more importantly, it can prevent it from coming back: kids get better and stay better.

As a clinician, I'm thrilled to know there's an effective alternative to medications. While some children may need to take medication just long enough to alleviate their symptoms so they can participate in treatment, this approach is not typically the first line of defense.

Fact: CBT treatment for children with diagnosable anxiety disorder is effective in 85% of cases. The benefits are maintained over time.

Play-based CBT

Children intuitively know that simply talking about the problem isn't enough. In fact, during therapy, children are the first to tell me if the "talk part" has gone on too long. They won't hesitate to ask, "How is this going to help me, anyway?"

Play is the natural language of children; toys and games are their lexicon. Children naturally need and want to engage through movement, fantasy and games, making play their greatest tool for growth and connection. Without play, children are robbed of the ability to process, explore and make sense of a difficult and confusing world, and to express their experience within it. Simply put, a child without play is a child who cannot thrive.

Play-based CBT blends two of the best tools to help children feel better and build resilience: play (essential for brain development) and CBT (essential for changing maladaptive thoughts and behaviors).

Traditional CBT is widely used with adults and adolescents who can learn to articulate what they are thinking and feeling, but the same tasks can be difficult for younger kids to perform because their brains have not yet developed the ability to process complex concepts into words. Traditional CBT can feel like "homework" to children. Without play and creativity in the mix, children shut down and disengage, making the whole endeavor frustrating for parents who so badly want to help.

Bringing play-based CBT into your home

Play-based CBT is solution-focused, so it provides meaningful ways to connect with our thoughts and feelings, change our way of looking at them and the behaviors that result and thereby create long-term positive changes. But perhaps its biggest selling point is that play-based CBT arms caregivers with tools that actually work and can be implemented outside of a clinical setting. And our role as parents and caregivers is critical because it offers the potential for success that therapy alone cannot match. The parent-child relationship is the biggest catalyst for building resilience and happiness.

Fact: With their parents' help, children as young as 2 or 3 years old can learn how to use non-anxious self-talk and confront fears through gradual exposure.

Bringing play-based CBT into family life addresses three of our children's fundamental needs: to communicate in their natural language, to share with trusted family members how they think and feel about themselves, and to master concrete tools that can help them change the thoughts and behaviors that feed their anxiety. Many of the activities in this book can be used with preschoolers through to adolescents and can be adapted for use at home, in the car and at school—wherever anxiety rears its head. There really are no hard-and-fast rules about how to integrate play-based CBT into family life, but having some consistency about how and when these tools are incorporated into daily activities is the best way to help children gain momentum in overcoming their anxiety and build on their successes.

Here are five tips from parents who have successfully used this technique:

1. work towards deepening your own self-understanding first
2. focus on the quality of your connection with your children

3. practice these tools during relaxed moments (rather than waiting for a crisis)
4. monitor the patterns in children's anxious behavior, especially noting any changes as they try new tools
5. expect success by persevering through your setbacks and celebrating your wins

I'd add that when using these tools, always remember to *soothe* before providing *support*. Soothing the emotional upset first reassures kids that we are present and builds the trust that allows them to be open to our support. It also bolsters our children's ability to use both logic and emotion to solve problems.

The beautiful, brilliant brain

The human brain is the most fascinating and complex organ in our body: it's the control center for everything from blinking, breathing and moving to thinking, learning and feeling. To embrace the benefits of play-based CBT, it's helpful for both parents and children to have a solid grasp on what the brain is, how it works and how anxiety affects it.

As incredibly complex as the brain is, children typically love to hear about how it affects their behavior and emotions. Many children also like to make sculptures and drawings of the brain and label its various parts, including the mid-prefrontal cortex and the brain stem. When we teach our children about their brain, they can see and better understand what is happening when they experience anxiety or fear, and they can also see how their anti-anxiety toolkit helps their brain to manage those emotional responses.

How you explain the concepts will depend on the age of your child. Don't worry if you find yourself revisiting the ideas over and over; it can take time for children to learn this new terminology. However, soon they'll be thrilled to call themselves "brain scientists." The Hawn Foundation's MindUp and CHI Kids and other programs delivered through schools are already equipping many children with the language they need to understand what is going on in their body and brain. The result is a whole generation of children talking about "taming their amygdala" and "taking a mindful moment." So don't be surprised if your children already have some basic understanding of this material or, if after learning this information, they blame their amygdala after a nasty outburst!

Talking to your child about the brain and anxiety

A good way to think of the brain is like a super computer that stores and processes information (like memories) for the future. The *limbic system* is a series of structures, including the *amygdala* and the *hippocampus,* that initiate emotions and impulses from deep inside the brain. All this reacting and feeling is regulated by the thinking brain, or the *prefrontal cortex.* Therefore, to manage stress and anxiety we can use the problem-solving abilities of the prefrontal cortex to identify the source of the stress and to train our brain to respond mindfully to it. Doing this makes us more self aware, puts us in charge of managing our own anxiety and leads to greater happiness overall.

To better understand what's happening in the brain, it's helpful to know a bit more about the amygdala, the hippocampus and the prefrontal cortex and how they work together.

The amygdala is no bigger than an almond, but despite its small size it plays a very important role in how we experience our emotions and how we receive and process incoming information. It also plays a role in how we react to fear and stress. The amygdala makes it possible for us to react to danger even before we know what that danger is by charging up our "fight, flight, freeze or dive" response.

The amygdala's important safety messages are "hardwired" into our brain so that when we come across a dangerous situation we can react quickly. For example, we automatically know to jump out of the way if a car is veering in our direction, or we know to

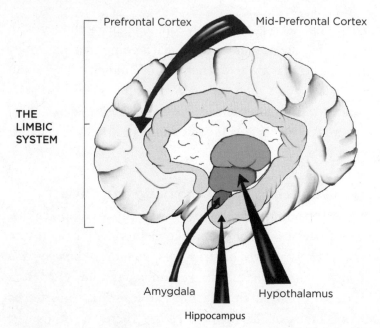

Prefrontal Cortex   Mid-Prefrontal Cortex

THE LIMBIC SYSTEM

Amygdala   Hypothalamus

Hippocampus

freeze and stay behind the railings when we are on a high bridge. However, there are times when our amygdala may overestimate just how dangerous a situation is. When that happens, we feel so anxious and uncomfortable that our fight, flight, freeze or dive response gets in the way. Our amygdala triggers a release of brain chemicals resulting in so many impulses that our prefrontal cortex cannot process them all quickly enough to solve the problem. Luckily, there are ways to "override" any incorrect messages we get from the amygdala.

The hippocampus is the part of the brain that helps us to remember things. This part of our brain helps us to manage fear by searching our memories to figure out if we really need to be scared in a certain situation, and if so, whether we have successfully used a particular approach to survive a similar predicament in the past.

Our prefrontal cortex is the decision-making part of the brain and it helps us choose actions that are appropriate for a particular time and place. Our hippocampus and prefrontal cortex work

Sample script: Explaining the fight, flight, freeze or dive response

Imagine that together we've discovered a time machine that can take us to whatever year we want. In a moment, it will be your turn and you can take us to any time in history, but for now I'd like to push some buttons and take us to two million years ago. Here we go...

Let's stay inside the time machine to keep ourselves safe. There are all kinds of dangerous creatures out there. Instead, let's look out the window and see what it's like for the cave dwellers who live here. What do you see?

I see a caveman looking for roots and berries. He seems pretty happy with all the berries he's finding. Uh oh...he won't be happy for long. There's a big tiger lurking in the bushes. What's the caveman going to do?

▸ Fight, by kicking and hitting at the tiger as it attacks?
▸ Flight, by running away as fast as he can?
▸ Freeze, by staying as still as he can so the tiger loses interest?
▸ Dive, by dropping to the ground and pretending he's dead?

(Allow your child to decide which of the responses the caveman chooses. They all come from the same part of the brain.)

It looks as if his amygdala saved his life! His reaction worked and he survived the dangerous attack. Thank goodness he has that really important part of his brain to tell him when there's danger. Now, let's travel back to the present and you can decide what time in history we're going to next!

together to help us calm down; as a team they can override the amygdala with activities like mindfulness and deep breathing (see chapter 6). These activities help us relax by slowing down our heart rate, lowering our blood pressure and increasing our focus on the present moment. This sends a message to our brain system that we are not in danger, and we do not need to enter into our "fight, flight, freeze or dive" mode. The more we practice progressive relaxation or deep breathing to calm down, the more we strengthen those pathways in our brain and move towards being calm and happy.

The neurotransmitters (or brain chemicals) *cortisol* and *dopamine* play important roles too. They are present in our brain at all times, but their levels fluctuate. When their levels are balanced, we feel calm, relaxed and alert, but when our cortisol levels are chronically too high, we begin to feel down. The low feelings cortisol brings are especially potent when the levels of our feel-good chemicals (like serotonin and dopamine) are low.

The body's autonomic nervous system is another key player when it comes to regulating stress. It is connected to the heart, lungs, stomach, intestines, bladder and sex organs and controls most of the unconscious, involuntary functions in the body, such as heart rate, breathing rate and sweating. It is made up of three parts: the sympathetic, parasympathetic and enteric nervous systems. While the *sympathetic* nervous system activates the fight, flight, freeze and dive reaction, the *parasympathetic* nervous system calms the body and brings it back into equilibrium. The parasympathetic nervous system is constantly slowing down our heart rate, managing our digestion and storing energy to counter the fluctuations of our sympathetic nervous system.

Our adrenal glands may be tiny, but they have an enormous job when it comes to regulating our body's response to stress. They produce stress chemicals like cortisol and noradrenaline that signal we're in peril, but because our adrenals can't differentiate

Brain discussion guide

1. Prompt a discussion with the following questions:
   a) How does the amygdala keep us safe? (*Answer:* It sends alarm messages to our body.)
   b) Can you remember a time when you were really scared or stressed and you couldn't think clearly? What do you think was happening in your brain?
   c) What's the secret to calming down *your* brain system?
   d) What alarm signals does your body use to tell you it's under stress? (*Answer:* racing heart, sweaty palms, frustration, distracted mind, etc.)
2. When children are fearful, anxious or angry, ask which part of the brain is working the hardest. If it's the amygdala, ask how it feels and what allows it to settle down. As an alternative, when you're aware of feeling frustrated or anxious, let your children know about it. ("I can really feel my amygdala getting in the way...I'm going to take some deep breaths to settle it down!")
3. Invite your children to play a brain science game of "Who am I?" Ask them to act like the amygdala, prefrontal cortex or hippocampus, and have the family guess which part of the brain they're pretending to be. They might run around in flight mode as the amygdala, appear thoughtful and pensive as the hippocampus or talk away their stress as the prefrontal cortex.
4. Set up a plan with your children for the next time the amygdala triggers an overreaction. Find out which calming strategy your children like the most and plan to use it. Most parents are quick to admit that their amygdala sometimes causes them to overreact too, so make this a household commitment!

between real danger and elevated stress, they can become fatigued, which compromises their ability to support our immune system and interferes with our overall health.

Knowing how to identify anxiety is hard enough for adults, let alone for children. The amygdala meter is a scale that can help children to understand and articulate the physical symptoms and severity of their anxiety. Knowing what to do to keep themselves in the green (or calm) zone also gives them a greater sense of control. Explaining how the amygdala works, why it gets revved up and what to do when it does can help kids to manage their stress levels. Keep in mind, the amygdala meter is not about the amygdala only. It is about the whole set of linked areas in the brain system.

THE AMYGDALA METER

Good for all ages

Materials needed: paper and pens or pencils

Our amygdala takes in information about the world around us and triggers a complex set of brain responses to cope with stress. The prefrontal cortex helps manage stress with important brain processes like planning, focusing and problem-solving. When the brain system is in a steady state, we are in the *green zone* and our body feels calm and relaxed. We're alert, focused and aware of our surroundings. This is the "just right" zone where we feel most comfortable.

Below the green zone is the *purple zone*. This is the zone we're in when we're tired or sick and we have low energy and might feel a little down. Being in this zone right before bedtime is okay, but it's not so great when we need to concentrate at school. At those times, we can bring our brain back into the green zone again by drinking a glass of water or taking a quick walk to get feel-good chemicals moving a little.

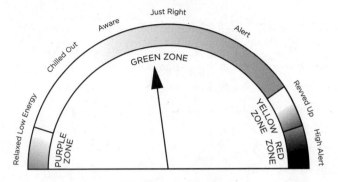

AMYGDALA METER

Online extra: The amygdala meter

The amygdala meter is very useful to help measure how your child is thinking and feeling while you're working through the exercises in chapter 6. Create your own meter at home or download a full-color version to print out and keep from michelekambolis.com/resources.

A little higher than the green zone is the *yellow zone*. We move into the yellow zone when we get revved up and feel a bit nervous and stressed. Going into this zone can be helpful when we have to give a presentation or if we're preparing for a soccer game because it keeps us alert. However, if we stay in this zone too long or go there at the wrong times, we can slip into fight, flight, freeze or dive mode. Remembering to breathe deeply can help to bring us back to the green zone.

If we aren't able to bring our brain system back to the green zone, it might go all the way to "high alert" and hit the *red zone*. This is when our amygdala is sharing so much information that the prefrontal cortex can't process it all. When we're in this zone, we feel really upset, scared or angry and our heart beats quickly or we become hot and sweaty and sometimes we even feel like we can't breathe. It can feel really scary to be in the red zone, so it's important to learn how to get back to the green zone.

Here are some strategies for returning to the green zone:

- do some square breathing (page 126)
- try progressive relaxation (page 144)
- visualize a peaceful scene
- think about a safe place
- do some yoga poses
- listen to calm music
- go for a walk
- repeat coping statements such as "I can do this, I have help, I'm not alone, I am safe right now"
- talk to someone you trust (encourage kids to talk to an adult who can help be their emotional processor)
- notice the surroundings and focus on the present

THE DOPAMINE METER
Good for all ages
Materials needed: paper and pens or pencils
Anyone who struggles with stress is prone to lower levels of dopamine and serotonin, the chemicals in the brain associated with feeling good and calm. The cool thing is that there are many ways to boost these feel-good chemicals, from social interaction to exercise. Even certain foods, such as almonds, avocados and bananas, can increase dopamine levels in the brain. Getting plenty of sleep and reaching a new goal are also known feel-good chemical boosters. We can help our children to stimulate those good feelings by encouraging behaviors that trigger the brain's release of the brain chemicals that support them best.

Kids love the idea that getting a hug or smelling an apple pie can make their brain surge with feel-good chemicals. Create a dopamine meter together by listing all the things that increase their feelings of happiness. They can turn to this tool for ideas to

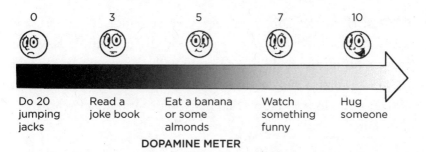

0	3	5	7	10
Do 20 jumping jacks	Read a joke book	Eat a banana or some almonds	Watch something funny	Hug someone

DOPAMINE METER

lift their mood at times when they are feeling anxious or when life is weighing them down. Keep in mind, the dopamine meter is about all the chemicals in the brain associated with feeling good.

STEP 1: On a piece of paper, draw a meter that goes from zero to ten. Explain that this meter measures the level of dopamine: the farther along the scale to 10, the higher the level of feel-good chemicals in their body and the calmer and happier they feel.

STEP 2: On a second sheet of paper, brainstorm a list of activities that boost the production of feel-good chemicals in the body. Here are some suggestions:

- hug someone
- play your favorite sport
- listen to happy music
- play with a pet
- watch a funny video
- go for a walk outside
- look at photos of a happy event in your life
- eat a healthy snack

STEP 3: Beside numbers zero, three, five, seven and ten, invite your child to create a feeling face that shows a range of feelings from extremely unhappy (zero) to extremely happy (tcn). Write one mood-boosting activity next to each emoticon.

STEP 4: Hang the dopamine meter where children can access it easily. Check the meter once a day, and discuss with kids where they are at on the scale. If necessary, talk about some strategies they might use to find balance. Remind them that they can always add new activities and tools that help them naturally increase their dopamine.

> PARENTING TIP: Using this tool is an excellent way to start a discussion with children about what's going on inside their brain when they are feeling overwhelmed. It also provides an opportunity to talk about what they're thinking and feeling, with the kind of loving connection that so naturally boosts their mood. Steer the conversation towards some of the tools for reducing stress and anxiety.

Learning to spot the signs of anxiety

Helping kids to recognize the feelings, thoughts and behaviors associated with their anxiety can help them to see how their body and brain try to survive their sometimes real but mostly imagined dangers. Older children can complete these checklists on their own; younger children can answer questions about their symptoms while an adult fills in the forms for them. Find print-ready versions of these worksheets at michelekambolis.com/resources.

Anxiety Checklist—Body

Anxiety is the opposite of feeling relaxed in the body. The following is a list of symptoms that some kids feel when they're stuck in anxiety mode. Put a check mark next to any problem that has bothered you during this past week, and indicate in the boxes on the right how commonly the symptom occurs for you.

PHYSICAL SYMPTOMS	NEVER	SOMETIMES	OFTEN
Sweating			
Headaches			
Dizziness			
Nausea			
Feelings of choking			
Ringing in the ears			
Redness in the face			
Dryness in the mouth			
Lump in the throat			
Feeling too hot			
Feeling too cold			
Shortness of breath			
Rapid breathing			
Racing heart			
Tightness in the chest			
Tingling lips			
Grinding teeth			
Weight loss			
Weight gain			
Constipation			
Diarrhea			
Stomachaches			
Butterflies			
Skin problems			
Lack of appetite			
Shaking			
Numbness or tingling in the limbs			
Jelly legs			
Muscle aches			
Pain			
Tension			
Difficulty falling asleep			
Insomnia			

Anxiety Checklist—Thoughts

Here's a list of thoughts that some kids have when they are feeling anxious. Put a check mark next to the anxious thoughts that have bothered you during this past week.

THOUGHTS	EXAMPLE	OCCURRED IN THE PAST WEEK
Obsessive thoughts	"I'm always worried about strangers trying to talk to me."	
Negative thoughts about yourself	"I can't do anything right. I'm so stupid."	
Unrealistic expectations of yourself	"I need be perfect. I'm not allowed to fail."	
Worst-case scenario thoughts	"I bet I got all the questions wrong and now I'm going to fail."	
"What-if" thoughts	"What if the doctor says I have cancer?"	
Self-harm/Suicidal thoughts	"Everyone would be happier if I weren't here."	
Negative comparisons of yourself to others	"She is so much prettier than me. I'm so ugly."	
Mind-reading thoughts	"I got the answer wrong. Now everyone thinks I'm stupid."	
Overblown thoughts	"This is the WORST thing that could happen."	
Unfounded conclusions	"She didn't answer my call so she must be mad at me."	
Unrealistic thoughts about situation	"I should get all A's in school. Getting a B means that I am a failure."	
"I can't" thoughts	"I can't do this, it's too hard."	
Negative thoughts	"Everything is going wrong today."	
Exaggerated thoughts	"If I don't score a goal, I'm a lousy soccer player."	
Self-doubting thoughts	"I don't think I will be able to pull this off."	
Self-blaming thoughts	"It's always my fault."	

Anxiety Checklist—Behaviors

Here's a list of behaviors that some kids experience when they are feeling anxious. Put a check mark next to the symptom or problem that has bothered you during this past week, and indicate how often it comes up for you.

BEHAVIORS	NEVER	SOMETIMES	OFTEN
Avoiding things you are supposed to do			
Following all the rules as strictly as possible			
Putting off doing things			
Doing things to get people's attention			
Needing more cuddle time than usual			
Checking for signs of danger			
Planning escape routes			
Eating more than your tummy says you need			
Not wanting to eat much			
Making yourself sick after eating			
Feeling very irritable			
Feeling angry and lashing out at people			
Sleeping more than usual			
Sleeping less than usual			
Hiding away from people			
Hurting yourself on purpose			
Skipping school			
Ignoring problems			
Getting annoyed with yourself			
Getting other people to do things for you			
Taking out your feelings on others			
Bottling up your anxious feelings			
Stuttering			
Talking more quickly or slowly than usual			

BEHAVIORS	NEVER	SOMETIMES	OFTEN
Pacing			
Being unable to sit still			
Leaving things unfinished			
Crying			

Interpreting the data

Taking note of our children's triggers, physical symptoms, behaviors and thought patterns helps put many pieces of a complex puzzle of information in place. And when kids sense that we are tuning in to what they are thinking and feeling, they are deeply reassured. Monitoring what our children's instinctual brain is trying to tell them can help identify which strategy to use to combat the resulting anxiety. And the more they become familiar with all the ways in which their amygdala and other parts of the brain system are communicating with them, the more they learn a whole new language for self-discovery.

I strongly encourage you to jot down the shifts and changes you see in your children while working with the play-based CBT tools in this book. Start by completing the anxiety checklists on pages 71 and 72 to create a baseline. As you work through the CBT tools, use the behavior log on page 75 to document patterns in your children's behavior. (Find a print-ready version of this worksheet at michelekambolis.com/resources.) You may also want to revisit the checklists from time to time to see how your kids are progressing. Change takes time, and it's easy to overlook just how far they have come. Measuring that change in an objective and undeniable way can motivate us enough to stick with the strategies.

The Behavior Log

BEHAVIOR	DATE	TIME	ENVIRONMENT	WHAT HAPPENED FIRST?	HOW DID I MEET THE EMOTIONAL NEED?	WHAT TOOL WAS USED?	WHAT WAS THE EFFECT?
Wouldn't go into classroom	Jan 8	8:45 A.M.	School	Emma's favorite friend wasn't at school yet.	Forgot to meet the emotional need.	Asked what thinking trap might be getting her amygdala going.	She said, "I don't know" and started to cry. I hugged her. Friend arrived and she calmed down.
Clung to mom's leg	Jan 9	8:55 A.M.	School	We were running late.	"I know it's hard when we're running late. It's stressful when we race to school like that. Is that what's upsetting you?"	"Asked if she'd do some square breathing (page 126) with me to settle down her racting heart."	Didn't try it at first but eventually did square breathing.

The Mood Meter

When kids are not able to communicate their level of anxiety in words, the mood meter can provide useful insight into their thoughts and feelings and help kids see if they're getting into dangerous territory.

On a recent ski trip, I saw dozens of kids standing in the ski camp lineup. A small nine-year-old girl was shivering and silently crying as she scanned the kids around her and looked at her father for reassurance. I then overheard the following conversation:

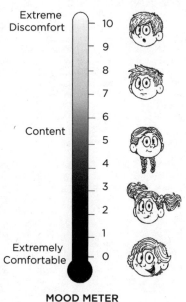

MOOD METER

FATHER: "What's wrong, are you cold?"

DAUGHTER: "No, my tummy hurts."

FATHER'S FRIEND: "What did you have for breakfast?"

FATHER: "I think you ate too fast. Just wait and you'll feel better soon."

DAUGHTER: "My tummy really hurts, though!" (She cries harder.)

FATHER (to his friend): "I don't think she's going to do this. I'm really sorry, it looks like I'm going to have to ski with her today."

FATHER'S FRIEND: "Don't worry about it. You do whatever you need to do."

FATHER (to his daughter): "Are you sure you're not okay? You always have a tummyache after you eat too fast, but it goes away."

DAUGHTER: "No, Daddy, it's not better." (And she cries even harder.)

Eager to ski, this dad missed an opportunity to tune in to his daughter's distress and to help her soothe herself through their parent-child attachment. Instead, he focused on the symptom rather than the core problem. She was terrified of ski school—that was easy to see in the way she scanned the faces of the children around her to determine whether they too were afraid. As her father misread her signals, she became more distressed, as if to say, "You're not seeing me. I'm alone in this fear."

Here's what this father-daughter interaction might have looked like, had they used the mood meter.

FATHER: "It looks like you're really upset. Can you tell me a little about what you're feeling?"

DAUGHTER: "My tummy really hurts."

FATHER: "Ouch. Your tummy hurts? If ten is the most hurt you can imagine, zero is your tummy not hurting at all and five is a medium amount of hurt, what number of hurt are you feeling?"

DAUGHTER: "I'm not sure. I think it's a seven."

FATHER: "A seven is a lot of hurt! Our tummy can hurt for a lot of reasons: sometimes we ate too fast or we're sick with flu. Or we're scared or nervous. Do you think your tummy hurts for any of those reasons?"

DAUGHTER: "I don't know. It just hurts."

FATHER: "Ski school is new for you, and sometimes when we try something new we can feel really anxious and our tummy can hurt. Could that be part of it?"

DAUGHTER (bursts into tears): "Why do I have to go to ski school? I really don't want to go. I want to ski with you, Daddy."

In my dream version of this scenario, I see the dad tuning in to his daughter's emotional reality. I imagine him taking the time to let her talk, and I see his active listening soothing her brain system, which is falsely telling her that ski school is as dangerous as a saber-toothed tiger. Perhaps she begins to calm down and is able to think of a solution as her father reminds her of all her calming-down tools. Maybe she starts to change her self-talk as she realizes she's tried new and scary things before and managed just fine.

In this version, Dad then bridges the attachment gap by talking with his daughter's instructor and allows the instructor to reassure her by explaining all the cool things they'll do together. Dad also reassures his daughter that he'll check in with her at lunchtime to see how it's going. I picture her little body calming down, her breathing slow and her face soften, as Dad checks the mood meter again. When he asks, "What number are you feeling now in your tummy?" she answers, "I think it's a four." Dad knows a four is manageable and sends her off on her ski day knowing that she feels safe and that her dad sees her wholly.

Motivating children

When children begin to face their fears, they need lots of validation and insightful conversation about their experience. Don't wait for consecutive successes before you point out the growth;

instead, check in with kids about what changes they are noticing and point out specific examples of recent situations where they have coped well. Drawing attention to their successes while letting less graceful moments slide will go a long way towards disempowering the anxious behavior. It takes several weeks for the brain to adapt to a new way of thinking and for a behavior to change, so remain patient and consistent while that's happening. Just because you don't yet see results, that doesn't mean positive change isn't taking place.

Remember, too, that negative self-talk can work against efforts to change a pattern of behavior. Teaching children strategies for managing anxiety is an important part of reducing it, but changing the mindset that produces it can be more difficult. Encourage children to look at what they *can* "do" and their mindset will surely follow. Every positive thought will propel them in the right direction. And support them by allowing them to conquer their fears one at a time by mastering a new step before introducing another challenge. Expect that managing the anxiety might get a little harder before it gets better; whenever we attempt to change a pattern of behavior, our innate need for consistency pushes back. It's only once we see repeated success with our new coping mechanism that we begin to trust that we can really let the old one go.

CONVERSATION STARTERS

Children often back away from conversations about their anxiety. Instead of pushing the topic, draw on their courage and imagination to give them the sense of safety they need to explore their feelings. Use these questions as a starting point:

▸ Imagine that your anxious feelings were hanging out with you for a while and that you could talk to them. What would you tell them about what you like and don't like about them?

▶ Imagine that you had the power to tell your anxious feelings and fears to go away—and they listened. What would you do that you aren't able to do now?

▶ Imagine that your anxious feeling or fears were an animal. What animal would they be? If you want, I can be that animal and you can wrestle me to the ground!

▶ Tell me about one of the first times you remember feeling afraid. What did you do to get through it?

▶ Imagine that courage was a color. What color would your courage be? Would you like me to put a string of that color around your wrist to remind you that you have brave feelings?

Parents often ask me if kids should be rewarded for facing their fears or practicing their tools. After working with thousands of kids in CHI Kids classes and in my clinical practice, I've found that tangible rewards are completely unnecessary for success. Children need to feel safe emotionally within themselves (and with you) to overcome their anxiety, and earning a prize cannot fulfill that need. Furthermore, anxious children who often have an internalized negative irrational belief that they "aren't good enough" are made to feel worse when they don't earn their reward. If you're highly attached to the idea of tangible motivators, create a box with bubble wands, squeezable stress balls, pinwheels and balloons, and buttons with catchy phrases like "Keep calm and carry on" that remind kids of their play-based CBT tools. This can be a way to reinforce the idea that caring for themselves is fun, but absolutely *do not* (and I rarely say these words) attach the prizes to success. The only motivation for practicing their tools is simple and natural: they want to spend fun, connected time with you while learning new ways to explore, grow and feel better inside.

SIX

THE PLAY-BASED TOOLBOX

The play-based CBT tools in this section can bring lasting relief to kids who learn and master them. How long it takes to do this will depend on many things: how old your children are, how deeply entrenched the anxiety thoughts and behaviors are, how consistently you work at learning and using these tools and what mindset *you* bring to the practice space. Parents of anxious children often inherently feel responsible for not doing enough or not having the answers, and we can feel guilty about having anxiety ourselves. Remember that any step towards healing is a positive step and even small changes can lead to big growth.

Don't worry if it takes many weeks to work through a single skill set; after all, it can take time for children to learn to fight against a long-held, instinctual response to danger. Reminding ourselves of our intention to bring joy into our parenting relationship with our children will draw us closer to them as we explore and practice new ways of communicating with ourselves and with our kids.

Whether these activities are used one on one, in groups or with the entire family, they are designed to bring children and adults together. And while it's helpful to begin by learning these tools together, ultimately the goal is to be able to call on them independently to prevent anxiety, treat symptoms as they arise and increase resilience and overall happiness. As with any healthy habit, aim to make this a daily personal practice and introduce new tools as previous ones are mastered.

Tools for mastering thoughts

Anxiety itself isn't the enemy. In many cases, our friend the amygdala is just letting us know that we're in a situation in which we might need to be on high alert, such as when a dog is barking at us or a car is too close. But it can also ring the alarm bell at all the wrong times, and when that happens the friend becomes a foe. We need to question the validity of its messages and take away its power step by step. Once our children recognize the situations in which that bothersome friend tends to ring a lot, they'll be better able to determine whether they're facing a real threat or a false alarm.

Everyone has thinking traps, or what psychologists call "cognitive distortions." Thinking traps are irrational beliefs that we hold on to without being aware of it, and they play a big role in reinforcing anxiety. By understanding the various types of thinking traps, we can better help our children identify and correct problematic patterns in their thinking. Many children have several recurring thinking traps, so in time it becomes easier to recognize them when they crop up. Thought leader Marianne Williamson wisely tells us, "You must learn a new way to think before you can master a new way to be." With self-awareness, children can learn to track their own thinking traps and mentally reframe their thinking in a more adaptive, positive way.

Many of the tools in this book rely on a basic understanding of the most common anxiety-related thinking traps, so it's helpful to study them before moving on to the interactive exercises. To make the concepts more accessible to children and to better illustrate how the thinking traps operate in real life, they are cast here as characters—our Thinking Trap Culprits.

Getting to know the Thinking Trap Culprits

Each Thinking Trap Culprit has its own M.O.—that's detective talk for "modus operandi," which means a habitual way of behaving. The M.O. is the culprits' way of trying to help us, but their efforts actually make things worse. By understanding how they work, we can neutralize their harmful actions and replace them with more positive ones.

Using the Thinking Trap Culprit ID cards as a reference, read through the descriptions of each culprit together to get a sense of who you might be encountering and what strategies can be used to defeat their M.O.

Thinking Trap Culprit

#1

All or Nothing ANDY

ONLINE EXTRA:

Download your own set of Thinking Trap Culprit ID cards to cut out and color from michelekambolis.com/resources

THINKING TRAP:
PERFECTIONIST THINKING

The culprit: All or Nothing Andy

The M.O.: For All or Nothing Andy, things are good or bad, perfect or terrible. They are either a complete success or a total failure. He is trying to help by pushing us to do our absolute best in every situation, but he is making things worse by demanding that things be perfect, which makes us feel like anything that isn't perfect is actually horrible.

Example: You sleep in, are late for school and exclaim, "The whole day is ruined."

To defeat the culprit:

▸ Thank All or Nothing Andy for wanting you to do your best. Let him know that it is okay to make mistakes.

▸ Do an imperfect job on a task deliberately, just to show All or Nothing Andy that it isn't the end of the world if you don't do everything perfectly.

▸ Question All or Nothing Andy's attitudes and see if you can make them more flexible. For example, try changing "The whole day is ruined because I slept in" to "I may have slept in, but I can make this moment great!"

THINKING TRAP:
DOOMSDAY THINKING

The culprit: Catastrophic Casey

The M.O.: Catastrophic Casey imagines the absolute worst thing that could possibly happen in any situation. She is trying to help by letting us know when we might be in danger, which would be useful if there was a fire in our house, but she tends to get confused and tells us we are at huge risk even when there is little chance of it.

Example: Your dad is driving you to school and you worry aloud, "Daddy, what if you're in a car accident?"

To defeat the culprit:

▸ Thank Catastrophic Casey for her efforts in keeping you safe.
▸ Remind Catastrophic Casey just how unlikely it is that her worry will ever come true.
▸ Let her know "It's not happening right now" and the only thing that's real and true is exactly what's happening in this moment.

THINKING TRAP: EXAGGERATED THINKING

The culprit: Eddie Exaggeration

The M.O.: Eddie Exaggeration tends to make small problems into *huge* ones. He sees things as far worse than they are and makes every task seem impossible. This is his way of trying to protect us from things that he believes will be difficult and stressful. Unfortunately, Eddie is making it harder for us to be successful by telling us that we are not good enough to do these things, or that these situations are gigantic and nothing can be done about them.

Example: You receive a poor grade on a test and state, "I'm the worst at math," or you have to clean up your room and exclaim, "This is going to take me all night!"

To defeat the culprit:

▸ Thank Eddie Exaggeration for trying to help and remind him that no problem is as big as he thinks.
▸ Tell yourself, "I can do this!"
▸ Start working towards your goal in small, manageable steps. Rather than thinking about cleaning your whole room, break it down into what you can do first, like cleaning off your desk.

THINKING TRAP:
SHOULD AND SHOULDN'T THINKING

The culprit: Shaun Should Pants

The M.O.: Shaun Should Pants thinks that every decision we make turns out to be a mistake. This is a popular culprit for children and adults alike! Shaun's strategy for dealing with stress is to tell us that we could have done better and that we need to be perfect. But instead of helping us to avoid disappointment, Shaun makes us feel *constantly* disappointed in ourselves.

Example: You feel nervous at the start of a new dance class and say, "I shouldn't feel so nervous all the time, what's wrong with me?" Or you have an argument with a friend and say, "I should have invited my other friend instead. I would have had a better time."

To defeat the culprit:

▸ Thank Shaun Should Pants for trying to point out a better choice.

▸ Remind him that regretting a decision doesn't mean you don't measure up.

▸ Tell yourself: "This is good enough for today. I might as well enjoy myself" and remind yourself that you can always make a different choice next time.

THINKING TRAP:
BLACK-AND-WHITE THINKING

The culprit: Always–Never Ever Amy

The M.O.: Amy sees things one way (black) or the other (white), with nothing in between (gray), and she likes to categorize situations into things that *always* happen and things that *never* happen, even if they actually happen only sometimes. Always–Never Ever Amy is trying to help protect us from scenarios we don't like, but she makes things worse by making us forget that the same situation could turn out just fine on another day.

Example: Your mom asks you to leave the room to calm down after a fight with your brother and you shout, "You *always* take his side!"

To defeat the culprit:

▸ Thank Always–Never Ever Amy for trying to help.
▸ Write, draw or think of a list of exceptions to Amy's all-or-nothing thinking.
▸ Remind Amy that there is such thing as "sometimes!"

THINKING TRAP:
LOOPBACK THINKING

The culprit: Mr. Vortex of Repetition

The M.O.: Mr. Vortex of Repetition thinks that if something happens once, it is bound to happen again and again. He tries to help us avoid disappointment by predicting what will happen in the future based on what has happened in similar situations in the past. Instead of making life better, though, he is stuck on the same story and makes things worse by creating negative expectations that are very hard to let go.

Example: You spill your drink at your favorite restaurant and tell your mom, "I don't want to go there anymore because I'm just going to spill my drink again."

To defeat the culprit:

▸ Thank Mr. Vortex of Repetition for trying to help.
▸ Remind Mr. Vortex that just because it happened in the past doesn't mean that it will happen in the future.
▸ Think about a time when a situation ended in disappointment once but went well the next time, and tell someone about it.

THINKING TRAP:
MIND READING

The Culprit: Mind-reading Mary

The M.O.: Mary adamantly believes that she knows what others *really* think—and it is almost always negative. Mind-reading Mary is trying to help by making sense of our surroundings, but she's making things worse by assuming that everyone around us is thinking negative things, which makes us feel as if the whole world is against us.

Example: You see a group of kids laughing in the playground and right away you assume they are laughing at you.

To defeat the culprit:

▸ Thank Mind-reading Mary for trying to help.

▸ Remind her that it is not possible to know what other people are thinking.

▸ Connect with what *you* think instead. Write a card to yourself and include in it what you like about yourself, including any compliments that you can think of. Seal up that card and save it for a time when Mind-reading Mary returns.

THINKING TRAP:
"IT'S ALL ABOUT ME" THINKING

The culprit: Me, The All-Powerful

The M.O.: Me, The All-Powerful assumes that everything is caused by him. He takes things personally and wants us to take the blame for everything. He feels stressed when other people are upset and so he is trying to make everyone feel better, but he is unfairly making us feel guilty for things we didn't do.

Example: Your mom overcooks the Thanksgiving turkey and you apologize, saying, "It's my fault. If I hadn't been distracting you, you would have been watching the turkey more closely."

To defeat the culprit:
- Thank Me, The All-Powerful for trying to help.
- Ask your parents to help you make a list of things that are your responsibility and things that are others' responsibility.
- Remind Me, The All-Powerful that it's okay to let others take responsibility for things, even when they make a mistake.

THINKING TRAP:
SKEPTICAL THINKING

The culprit: Blindfold Bob

The M.O.: Blindfold Bob minimizes all positive qualities or experiences and rejects positive feedback. He tells us not to trust compliments or good experiences. He is trying to help us by keeping our expectations low to avoid disappointment, but he goes overboard testing the truth of the compliments we receive and fills us with self-doubt.

Example: Your mom compliments you when you do well at track and field, and you say, "You're just saying that because you're my mom."

To defeat the culprit:
- Thank Blindfold Bob for trying to help.
- Remind Blindfold Bob "I am a worthwhile person and can be kind to myself."
- Remind him of your strengths; for example, "I really did do well at track and field today!"

THINKING TRAP:
"ISM" THINKING

The culprit: General Label

The M.O.: This culprit loves to attach labels to herself and others, generalizing a single flaw into an entire character. General Label is doing her best to try to help us by sorting and labeling information so we can understand it. Unfortunately, she's in a hurry and doesn't want to waste time and effort collecting all of the data, so she takes shortcuts in her thinking and makes hasty judgments. But she's only causing more harm than good by assigning inaccurate labels and making us and others feel bad.

Example: You complete the wrong page of homework and tell yourself, "I'm such a loser."

To defeat the culprit:

▸ Thank General Label for trying to help.

▸ Remind General Label that no one is perfect and that mistakes are only one part of our experience.

▸ Draw yourself in the middle of a piece of paper, and around you list all your thoughts, emotions and body sensations to let General Label know that you are aware and accepting of all of the parts of your experience, not just your flaws or mistakes.

THINKING TRAP:
BLAME THINKING

The culprit: Blame Blaster

The M.O.: Instead of trying to discover the cause of a problem, Blame Blaster quickly assigns blame. He is trying to help us feel less vulnerable by placing the blame on someone else, but he is forgetting to look at what has actually caused the problem. By jumping to conclusions, he makes things worse by making us and other people feel guilty.

Example: Your family cat has gone missing and you cry out, "It's Dad's fault. He probably left the door open again!"

To defeat the culprit:

▸ Thank Blame Blaster for trying to help you.

▸ Remind Blame Blaster that a problem does not need to have blame attached to it. After all, problems are a great chance for learning!

▸ Remind Blame Blaster that it's more helpful to look for real solutions when something goes wrong.

Learning to escape from thinking traps

Being aware of the many types of thinking traps brings us one step closer to developing realistic thinking. As parents, we are the key to helping our kids develop this critical skill. Through our help, our children's thoughts can reflect their hopes, not their fears. As we let them know that no thoughts are *bad,* we can reinforce the idea that there are helpful, unhelpful and neutral thoughts. To tell which is which, we might need to analyze them first, like a scientist.

Every scientist has a hypothesis, an idea that might be true although it hasn't been proven yet. We can invite our children to become thought scientists, using their keen powers of observation to gather data to prove or disprove their thought or hypothesis.

STEP 1: State the problem. Ask children to share a thought that makes them feel upset, anxious or worried. Encourage them to be as specific as possible. For example, "I'm scared because I have a test and I think I'm going to fail."

STEP 2: Formulate and test the hypothesis. Help the children to ask questions that might prove or disprove this thought. For example, asking why they think they're going to fail may lead straight to a Thinking Trap Culprit (check the list to see if any of them seems likely). If that's the case, move straight to Step 3. However, if they're not sure, you may want to try some of the following questions:

1. What thinking trap might you be in?
2. Have you faced this situation before?
3. Did something bad happen?
4. Has something bad happened every time you were in a similar situation?
5. What might have led to the upsetting outcome?
6. Are there other reasons why this could have happened?
7. Is there anything you could have done differently?
8. What else could happen in this situation?
9. What have other people done in this situation to have a better outcome?
10. What's the best-case scenario?
11. What's the worst-case scenario? What are the chances of that worst-case scenario occurring?
12. What's most likely to happen?
13. Could you cope with your worry if the worst-case scenario came true?
14. Are you underestimating your ability to cope with a poor outcome?
15. Can you control how this goes?
16. Are there things you can do to prepare?

STEP 3: Evaluate your results. With the kids, talk about whether the hypothesis still fits or whether there might be other reasons for their worry. Help them to identify an optimistic thought they'd like to attach to their worry, reminding them that what you choose to tell yourself every day can either lift you up or tear you down. For example, if Mind-reading Mary is telling them, "My friend doesn't like me and that's why he isn't coming to my birthday," help them see that there may be other reasons for their friend's decision. Phoning the friend might be an easy way to remove the cause of the worry.

STEP 4: Invite children to picture the situation in their mind while they repeat their optimistic thought.

PARENTING TIP: You've probably noticed that asking children questions when they're feeling anxious can shut communication down further and lead to the dreaded "I don't know" reply. If you stay curious and avoid directly disproving their negative hypothesis, you'll keep the communication more open. When they are anxious, children can hold steadfastly to their counterproductive theories, which can lead to a power struggle. Instead of jumping in with your own solutions, lead them gently through the hypothesis-testing process, allowing them to find their own way to a resolution. Use active listening, staying empathetic and repeating what they're telling you to be sure you understand correctly.

Tools for busting old thought patterns

Once they've identified and challenged their thinking traps, children are well on their way towards cognitive restructuring, the process of creating new pathways or thought patterns in the brain. The following Thought Busters are simple to use, and if used diligently they can be very powerful tools to combat anxiety and increase optimistic and adaptive thinking.

Brain "muscles" are just like any other muscle in their body. The more they flex, the stronger they'll become. Paying more attention to positive thoughts will build positive thought muscles, and in turn, ignoring negative thoughts makes negative thought muscles smaller and less powerful. Introduce these Thought Busters to your children and watch them grow stronger, more positive thought patterns.

BALLOON BUSTER

Good for all ages

Materials needed: balloons and a permanent marker

Most children will tell you the Balloon Buster is their favorite activity in the CBT toolbox: it's fun, cathartic and easy to do. Use this tool to turn things around when a child is in the grip of a thinking trap. In fact, some parents have been known to carry a bag of balloons with them for negative-thought emergencies.

STEP 1: Help children identify a negative belief that's contributing to their anxiety or discomfort. The negative belief usually starts with "I" (e.g., "I'm not good enough" or "I can't do it.")

STEP 2: Look through the list of thinking traps and help kids to determine which culprit might apply. This step helps them to discredit the negative belief and shows that it's simply inaccurate.

STEP 3: Encourage children to *let go* of the negative belief by breathing it out of the body and into the balloon. With each breath, they're making that negative belief smaller and leaving more room for empowering thoughts. (Keep in mind that some children have a hard time blowing up balloons, in which case you can set them up for success by doing it for them. Simply ask them to pretend they're blowing it up themselves.)

STEP 4: Leave the balloon untied; just have children pinch the opening closed with their fingers. For extra effect, write the negative belief on the balloon with a permanent marker. Tell them that they can get rid of the negative thought by releasing the balloon and letting it fly around the room. You'll probably notice them burst into laughter as they see the balloon (and their negative thoughts) fly out of control.

STEP 5: Next, help kids to identify an opposite, more helpful thought to replace the negative one. "I'm not good enough" becomes "I'm good enough just as I am" and "I can't do it" turns into "I can take it one step at a time."

STEP 6: Finally, have children close their eyes and inhale deeply, imagining that they are breathing that positive thought into their body, to take up the free space where the negative thought once lived.

BUBBLES BUSTER

Best for ages 5–10

Materials needed: bubble solution and wands

The Bubbles Buster not only helps children let go of negative thoughts, it also promotes deep breathing.

STEP 1: Help children to choose a recurring and counterproductive thought that makes them anxious or upset. Maybe they'd like to focus on letting go of a negative belief about themselves ("I'm not smart enough"), someone else ("My best friend doesn't like me anymore") or a situation ("School is going to be too hard to deal with").

STEP 2: Have them look through the Thinking Trap Culprit ID list (page 85) and pick the culprit their thought is connected to. For example, when you tell yourself, "My best friend doesn't like me anymore," you're dealing with Mind-reading Mary.

STEP 3: Encourage children to scan their body, starting at the top of their head and working their way down to the tip of their toes, and notice what emotions and sensations they feel when they hold that thought in their mind. Have them point to the places in their body where they experience those feelings the most.

STEP 4: Here's the fun part. Ask kids to fill their lungs, take a long, deep breath, and slowly blow out their unhelpful thought, negative emotions and physical sensations into the bubble wand. Watch that thought and the discomfort it causes float away, held safely inside the bubble. Better yet, pop those bubbles and negative thoughts right along with them. The more deep breaths kids take, the more bubbles they can blow and the better they'll feel.

STEP 5: Have children think of an optimistic thought they'd like to replace the old one and help them to picture what it might look like. Once they've pictured that new thought clearly, have them breathe it into their body.

STEP 6: Finally, have children do another body scan, noticing the emotions and sensations that have shown up now that the new thought is in their mind.

THE POSITIVE SWITCH

Best for ages 7–12

Materials needed: rubber/plastic bracelet or ring

The Positive Switch thought buster is a favorite with children who may be struggling with obsessive thoughts or "sticky thinking." It teaches them that, with practice, it's possible to change the channel. Since sticky thoughts are hard to see, it's virtually impossible for parents to know how often kids are battling them. But this tool can be used in the car or virtually anywhere and is a great way to monitor how often these types of thoughts are happening and what triggers them.

STEP 1: Start by explaining that having a flexible mind takes daily practice.

STEP 2: Give children a rubber band, bracelet or ring to wear. Let them know it's a symbol for their own superpower ability to create a flexible mind and a happy heart.

STEP 3: Encourage them to bring to mind a particular negative thought that sticks the most, a thought that often distracts them or interferes with their life. For example, a child with obsessive thoughts might be thinking, "I have to get all my homework done on Mondays or else I'll fail in school" or "I have to know where my mom is at all times or she'll have bad luck."

STEP 4: Now have them choose a reassuring and positive self-statement that makes them feel better. For example, "I have lots of time to get my homework done and I know I'll do just fine" or "My mom is an adult and can look after herself, so she doesn't need me to keep her safe." This statement is the bridge away from the sticky thought towards their flexible mind.

STEP 5: Ask kids to think about their sticky thought, then switch their bracelet (rubber band or ring) from one hand to the other at the same time as they say the positive self-statement out loud or in their mind.

STEP 6: Encourage them to switch the band from one hand to the other each time the sticky thought comes up. This way you'll know whether the sticky thoughts are increasing or decreasing.

THE SPONGE SQUEEZER
Good for all ages
Materials needed: a large sponge, a bucket of water, natural food coloring and a glass of drinking water (optional)
The sponge-squeezing thought buster is a great introduction to progressive relaxation, particularly for smaller children who may

find it difficult to focus on abstract images. This tool is especially helpful for kids going through a pushing or hitting phase, as squeezing the sponge releases body tension and helps kids regulate frustration and anger.

STEP 1: Have kids imagine their body is a sponge, and their body sponge can absorb thoughts and feelings that are helpful as well as ones that aren't.

STEP 2: Help them recall an unhelpful thought and feeling they often battle. For example, "This is a horrible day. I feel *so* sad" or "My sister always gets me in trouble. I feel really mad."

STEP 3: Take a big sponge and place it in a water bucket. Encourage kids to squeeze all of the water out of their sponge by using both hands. Let them know that as they're squeezing out all that water from the sponge, they're also squeezing all of that unhelpful thought and negative feeling out of their body and mind.

STEP 4: Invite them to fill the sponge with water and squeeze it out again (and again, if needed) until they've got all the water out of the sponge and all the negative thought and the sad, mad, scared or anxious feelings that went with it out of their body sponge. It's okay if it's not completely gone.

STEP 5: Help children to imagine a positive thought and a good feeling they'd like to bring into their mind and body instead.

STEP 6: Have children imagine the thought and feeling as a color, then use natural food coloring to magically turn a glass of water into drinkable thoughts and feelings of that color.

STEP 7: Invite kids to drink in their helpful thought and positive feelings to fully bring them in to their mind and body. Join in and you can all drink up the joy!

THE THOUGHT FREEZER

Good for all ages

Materials needed: an ice cube

When children are fixated on a distressing or negative thought, it can dart through their mind at lightning speed and capture all their mental attention. Using this exercise can help kids to stop the thought in its tracks. Then, rather than fixating on and deconstructing the thought, they can simply let go of it. This activity combines visualization (page 138) and mindfulness (page 130) and gives kids the opportunity to picture their negative thoughts as a tangible object that they can control. Use it anywhere there's ice and a place to connect.

STEP 1: Help kids to identify the negative or anxious thought that's overwhelming them. Ask them to picture that thought in their mind and order it to freeze.

STEP 2: Give them a piece of ice to hold in one hand and have them imagine their own negative thought locked up in it.

STEP 3: Describe a warm summer sun shining brightly right above the frozen negative thought. Have them squeeze their hand around the ice cube, and as the ice melts, encourage them to picture the negative thought melting away too. (The sensation of the ice turning into cool water dripping from their fingers helps bring their attention to the physical object, which they can feel getting smaller and smaller in their hand.)

STEP 4: As the negative thought melts away, ask children to replace it with a positive, self-affirming one. If you want, have them use a finger to gently trace the positive thought on the palm of the hand that was holding the ice.

THE WORRY WALL

Good for all ages

Materials needed: sticky notes, markers

Imagination is the most powerful tool kids have to conquer anxiety and the thoughts that fuel it. The Worry Wall thought buster lets children use their imagination and externalize those counterproductive worry thoughts by building walls that can be torn down "brick" by "brick." Make space—some of these walls can fill an entire kitchen or living room!

STEP 1: Introduce kids to this activity by letting them know that you've been thinking a lot about their worries and you have a special way to help get those worries out of their head. Some people imagine there's a "worry bug" that likes to munch on worries; the more worries that bug eats, the hungrier it seems to get. One way to block the bug from feeding on worries is by writing them down and sticking them on a "worry wall." They may want to include a solution if the worry is one that can be solved. Once those thoughts are on the worry wall they're no longer in our mind—the worry bug can eat the worries on the wall instead! Once the worries are out, the worry bug has nothing to eat and goes somewhere else.

STEP 2: Encourage children to write or draw as many worry thoughts as they can and stick all their worries on their very own worry wall. Remind them that once the worries have been written down, they don't have to think about them anymore.

STEP 3: Now here's the most important part: each worry needs a positive thought to replace it. Have kids build another wall—their optimism wall. For each worry, create two thoughts to replace it; make sure those new thoughts are optimistic ones. By the time the wall of optimism is finished, it will be twice as big as the worry wall!

STEP 4: Once children have built their optimism wall, invite them to go ahead and tear down their worry wall, munching up the papers in their hands just like the hungry worry bug.

> **PARENTING TIP:** Give children a stack of sticky notes to keep on hand for school, play dates or visits to the doctor or dentist. Then, whenever they need to, they can write down their worries. If they haven't yet torn down their worry wall, remind kids to leave this food for the worry bug on their wall when they get home.

WORRY TIME

Best for ages 5–10
Materials needed: an egg timer or clock with an alarm

Anxious children can spend an inordinate amount of time worrying, and this is time that could be better used for learning, playing and developing optimistic expectations. Dedicating a specific time of day to hold children gently in your arms and sit with them while they face their worries can go a long way towards strengthening your emotional connection and creating a safe container to hold whatever arises and passes through them. Trust and physical closeness trigger the release of the soothing hormone oxytocin, which leaves kids feeling calmer and more relaxed.

STEP 1: Introduce kids to this activity by letting them know you've noticed how much time their worry thoughts are taking up in the day and that you've learned a great way to curb the habit—Worry Time.

STEP 2: Help children choose a regular time of day to do their worrying, avoiding anytime within an hour of bedtime. Ideally, Worry Time should take place when you're readily available so they're not bringing up their biggest fear as you're racing out the door, late for an appointment.

STEP 3: Use an overt cue, such as playing a particular song or ringing a bell or flipping a light switch, to show that Worry Time has begun. Allow kids to choose to name their worries out loud or internally. Your job is to listen and allow those fears to exist in your presence.

STEP 4: As you come towards the end of Worry Time, help children create a plan to face their lingering fears or remind them of their thought-buster tools. Help shift the discussion to resilient thoughts they'd like to have in their mind instead. This is a good time to use their Personal Motto (page 255) or Care Tag (page 259).

STEP 5: Use your sound or light cue to signal that Worry Time is over and remind kids that if another worry thought pops up, they can simply remind themselves, "It's not the right time to worry. I can think about that problem during Worry Time." If they forget to worry about it later, it usually means it wasn't worth worrying about in the first place.

PARENTING TIP: Measure the length of children's Worry Time by their age. That is, Worry Time for five-year-olds is five minutes, and so forth. Feel free to adjust the worry time as needed, without allowing it to go on too long.

As an alternative to Worry Time, consider alternating one minute of worry with one minute of positivity. By switching from worry thoughts to positive ones, children learn just how capable their brain is of switching the thought channel.

THE HARD DRIVE CLEANUP

Best for ages 8–12

Materials needed: pens and paper, paints, inspiring images, a journal or music to inspire

While older children still benefit from our steady presence during Worry Time, many are ready to use their tools more independently when worries loom large in their awareness. Computer-loving kids will appreciate the metaphor in this exercise.

STEP 1: Introduce this activity by telling children that just like a computer, their mind only has a certain amount of storage space for data. It would be great if worries were attached to a file in our minds that we could simply delete, but sometimes they pile up, taking up too much storage space and leaving less room for all of the other functions our brain needs to perform. It can be helpful to take some time each day to go through those worries and "clean up your hard drive."

STEP 2: Help kids to imagine that each of the worries in their head is in its own file on their brain's hard drive. Let them know that you're going to open up those worry files and see which ones can be deleted.

STEP 3: Set a timer to go off after ten minutes or so, when the session will come to an end. Alternatively, you might create a ten-minute playlist of soothing instrumental songs to play in the background. Once the playlist is over, the hard drive cleanup is complete.

STEP 4: Invite children to ask themselves a few questions about each worry file as they open it:

1. What is this worry about?
2. How much does this situation affect my life now? How much will it matter in five years?
3. How much energy is the worry worth?
4. Is there anything I can do to change this situation? (Try to be as honest as possible. If the answer is no, then you know that no matter how much you worry about this problem, nothing will change.) Can I accept this situation?
5. Which part of this situation is within my control? Is there anything I can do right now? If so, what might that be?

STEP 5: Going through these questions helps kids to develop a better idea of how to deal with each worry file. If they find a solution, they can go ahead and mentally delete it. If it's a situation beyond their control, they can give themselves permission to accept what they cannot change and delete that file too. Some worry files are not solvable and may crop up again. Knowing this, children might want to make a list of mindfulness techniques they can use when dealing with this worry in the future. Choosing to be the watcher of their thoughts and behavior, finding stillness and quieting the internal noise can take them towards letting go.

STEP 6: As children reach the end of their hard drive cleanup, they should notice that they have a lot more free space that can be filled with something that brings them joy. Invite them to take five or ten minutes to "download" something more inspirational by listening to uplifting music, doing some journaling, or drawing or painting something that will fill the newly cleared space in their mind with positivity.

THE HICCUPS

Ages 6–12

Materials needed: slips of paper, a bag or shoebox, five jars, labels

For children battling anxiety, even small problems can feel huge and insurmountable. Learning to identify the difference between small-, medium- and large-scale problems will help them to develop a sense of perspective, which is an important antidote to feeling overwhelmed. This exercise helps children to sort their worries into categories, so they can weed out those not worth concerning themselves with and tackle the rest head-on. Choose twenty or so worries that you feel your children could identify with. Write them on slips of paper and go through them together.

STEP 1: Problems in life are a bit like the hiccups—they can be distracting and upsetting, but they are usually temporary and solvable. Copy these hiccups onto slips of paper ahead of time and put them into a bag or a shoebox. (If the children are young, omit any that you feel would be very upsetting or confusing to them. If the children are older, have them help you select and write out the hiccups.) Let kids know that the hiccups are safely stored away but that they need to be taken out one by one and put in their suitable place. That way, you can find out together which hiccups can be cured or dumped right away.

STEP 2: Find five jars and label them "Big Hiccups," "Medium Hiccups," "Small Hiccups," "Hiccup Dumpster" and "For Mom or Dad Only."

STEP 3: Take the hiccups out of the bag or shoebox one by one and help the kids figure out which category each one fits into.

The Hiccups

1. Your sibling takes your toy.
2. Your sibling breaks your Lego creation.
3. You spill something.
4. Your clothes get dirty.
5. You didn't get the teacher you wanted.
6. Your favorite friend isn't in your class.
7. Your favorite friend is away from school.
8. You lose a board game.
9. You don't get the grade you wanted on your test.
10. You have to give a presentation in front of the class.
11. Your teacher asks you to work in a group with people you do not like.
12. You have to eat your least favorite food for breakfast/lunch/dinner.
13. You have to ask the teacher for help when he/she seems busy.
14. You weren't able to complete your work at school, so now you have to take it home as homework.
15. Your soccer/baseball/hockey team has to play against a better team.
16. You aren't able to go on a play date.
17. You are not picked first for an activity.
18. You hear a strange noise outside your bedroom door at night.
19. You have a bad dream.
20. The person sitting next to you is being loud or disruptive.
21. You trip while walking down the street.
22. You have to get a needle when you go to the doctor.
23. It's raining outside so you have to be indoors all day.
24. There is a spider in your room.
25. You cannot sit where you want to at lunchtime.

26. You get into an argument with your friend.
27. You lose $20.
28. You did not finish your homework on time.
29. You forget your umbrella at home on a rainy day.
30. Your night-light goes out in the middle of the night.
31. Your computer crashes before you can save your work.
32. You have to ask someone for help at the store.
33. You're being teased or bullied at school.
34. You trip and fall down the stairs.
35. You get stuck in an elevator.
36. Your mom and dad don't live together anymore.
37. Your mom or dad starts to date other people.
38. You have to sleep in the dark.
39. You miss the bus to school.
40. The power goes out during a storm.
41. You fail a subject because you were unable to do the work.
42. You get separated from your safe adult in a public space (e.g., a shopping mall, amusement park, grocery store).
43. You get bitten by an animal.
44. A family relative dies.
45. Your family dog/cat gets lost.
46. You have to go to the hospital because you feel sick.
47. There's a fire in the kitchen when someone is cooking.
48. A big storm has damaged your home.
49. Your mom or dad got fired from a job.
50. A tragic event is reported in the news (e.g., a school shooting, terrorist attack).
51. You witnessed a crime taking place (e.g., hit and run accident, police chase).
52. You were hit, kicked or hurt by someone.
53. Your friend was in a serious accident and got hurt.

▸ A small hiccup is mildly annoying or frustrating but can be fixed by making a small change in plans. Small hiccups are temporary and will sometimes go away if ignored.

▸ Medium hiccups are harder to work around and usually it's not a good idea to ignore them. They are not very easy to get over and may take some time to adjust to.

▸ Big hiccups don't show up as often but they can really be serious.

▸ Some hiccups may be irrelevant for certain kids who haven't encountered a particular situation, and these ones can go straight into the Hiccup Dumpster.

▸ "For Mom or Dad Only" hiccups are really important. These ones are too big for kids to manage and should really be in the hands of adults. When children take on adult problems, their anxiety goes through the roof. Creating a concrete way to separate child-appropriate worries from adult problems can bring enormous relief.

STEP 4: Once the hiccups have been sorted into jars, start by looking one by one at the problems in the "Small Hiccups" jar. If you can solve the problem, move it to the "Hiccup Dumpster." As you acquire more tools for tackling hiccups, notice how few are left!

PARENTING TIP: Point out that hiccups can trick you. Sometimes a small problem can cause a big reaction. Notice if some small or medium hiccups might be trying to get into the "Big Hiccups" jar or even the "For Mom or Dad Only" jar. Talk through the real-world consequences and solutions to the hiccups, and help children to reevaluate if it seems that they are blowing some scenarios out of proportion. For help with big hiccup items, especially disproportionate fears or phobias, see page 118 for help with facing a hierarchy of fears.

THE CHAIN LINK

Best for ages 7–12

Materials needed: strips of paper, roll of tape, markers

This thought buster is a great way to show kids the link between their experiences, thinking patterns and their physical and emotional reality. Feel free to get creative by making thought-buster necklaces, bracelets or chain links that span the room!

STEP 1: Have kids write one negative situation they recently struggled with, on a strip of paper. For example, "My friend and I argued," "My brother broke my toy" or "My Dad got mad at me."

STEP 2: On a second strip of paper, have them write down the emotion that usually comes with that experience (sad, angry, scared, etc.)

STEP 3: On a third strip of paper, have them write down the negative thought that goes with the experience ("I did something wrong" or "I'll never forgive my brother") and how that negative thought affects their body (tense muscles, upset tummy, rapid heart rate, etc.)

STEP 4: On a fourth strip of paper, have them write down how that negative thought makes them behave (yell at their sibling, pace back and forth, withdraw from others, etc.)

STEP 5: Tape the ends of one strip to make a loop. Loop the second strip of paper through the first one and stick the ends together with tape. Continue with the other two strips of paper to form a chain of links. Repeat this process with any other negative thoughts they have on their mind.

STEP 6: Together, have fun breaking the chain by ripping the links apart. As you do, imagine that the negative thought, unwanted feeling, body response and behavior are no longer linked. Remind kids that *they* can decide whether they're chained by their thoughts, feelings, body responses or behaviors. Some children delight in crumpling up the ripped-up chain and tossing it in the trash.

STEP 7: Take a fifth and final strip of paper and write down the thought that is the opposite of the negative one (e.g., "I am a good person," "I am allowed to make mistakes," "I can forgive," etc.). On the same strip, write the emotion that goes with that positive thought (happy, relaxed, proud, etc.), the way that thought makes the body feel (relaxed muscles, calm heart, etc.) and the action they will take instead (smiling, talking calmly, etc.).

STEP 8: Finally, help kids make the strip of paper into a bracelet by taping it around their wrist with the message facing inward. The bracelet will help them remember their personal positive message and the behavioral choices that go with it. Encourage kids to repeat these positive intentions to themselves throughout the day; the more often they do, the better they'll manage emotionally, physically and behaviorally. And happiness will more naturally come from their actions.

WORRY CHARACTERS
Good for all ages
Materials needed: modeling clay or drawing materials
It can be hard for children to know sometimes where their anxiety ends and where they begin. Redefining their worry as a silly cartoon character that's interfering with their ability to see things clearly can help separate their sense of self from their powerful feelings and gives them a tool to access more control.

STEP 1: Introduce this activity by explaining that worry thoughts are like junk mail. They are messages you get that you don't want, and they can really pile up and make a mess.

STEP 2: Help kids to invent a name for the sender of the junk mail, such as Worry Bug, Mr. Stressed, etc. Remind them that, just like junk mail, the nuisance messages from this sender can be ignored as soon as they come in. There's no point in reading the message because it's false advertising and the sender doesn't know you. Instead, just throw it out right away.

STEP 3: Young children might find it fun to create their character using modeling clay, so they can give the character a voice, confront it or even squish it if it's really bugging them. Older kids can make a cartoon strip showing the character trying to outsmart them and the ways they regain control, push back and defeat the worry character.

BOSSING BACK

Best for ages 5–9
Materials needed: none

One way to help children feel more in control of their anxious thoughts is to "boss back" their Worry Character. This task gives them a chance to tell the part of their brain that puts them on high alert just how frustrated they are.

STEP 1: Begin this exercise by saying to kids that you've noticed their Worry Character has been getting really bossy lately. Sometimes when people are really bossy, we need to tell them exactly how we feel and stand up for ourselves.

STEP 2: Kids who have drawn a picture or made a figurine of the Worry Character can address it directly. Help children revive their feeling of being in charge by telling the Worry Character exactly what a nuisance it's become. Allow them to blow off steam and express their frustration to the Worry Character. One of the children I work with recently bossed back her Worry Character and here's what she had to say: "Stop bossing me around, Worry Face! You're not helping me right now. I don't like you! Come back when there's actually something to worry about. You bug me in the worst moments. When I'm trying to go to sleep, you tell me there's fleas in my bed . . . When I'm at home, you make me worry that my mom will get mad at me when I haven't done anything wrong . . . You make me feel bad, and I'm sick of it! I'm going to annihilate you by squishing you in my hands!"

> **PARENTING TIP:** The freedom to firmly and strongly talk back to their anxiety can be an incredibly powerful tool for children. Help them in "bossing back" their Worry Character by giving them some examples of firm commands, such as "Stop it now!, Go away!, I don't need you right now." You can also help kids learn the non-verbal aspects of being assertive. Encourage them to stand tall, use direct eye contact and puff out their chest.

THE HEART TOTEM

Good for all ages

Materials needed: small symbolic items, such as hearts made of felt

Children with separation anxiety often worry that something might happen to their caregivers in their absence. A transitional object can help symbolize your presence and bring attention to the power of your unbreakable bond rather than to the temporary separation.

STEP 1: Encourage children to make or decorate a pair of transitional objects, such as a pair of hearts made of felt. Explain that the hearts show your love and remind them that it's always with them, even when you're apart. You'll carry one of the hearts and your children will carry the other.

STEP 2: Whenever you say goodbye to each other, swap hearts. Let them know that when they want to feel your presence, they can take out the heart and hold it in their hand. They can use it as a reminder that they will be back with you soon. Tell them about an activity you can look forward to doing once you're together again.

STEP 3: When you are reunited, swap hearts again and take a moment to truly delight in your child's presence, discuss what happened while you were apart and take the time to engage in the promised activity.

PARENTING TIP: Objects that feel good to the touch, such as a soft felt heart or a smooth stone, make great choices because they allow children to be soothed by the material itself. This activity builds trust when you follow through with prompt pickup times and keep to your word by reconnecting mindfully, and kids feel far more in control, which helps to reduce their anxiety. Older children like to have a secret word that says, "You are what matters most to me and you have my heart." When either you or your children use that word, it reaffirms your connection and makes them feel safe and cared for.

FEAR-FIGHTING SPRAY

Best for ages 3–10

Materials needed: glitter, calming essential oils, glycerin, spray bottle, label

This tool instills in kids a sense of inner control and strengthens their belief that they are strong enough to face their anxieties and fears.

Common fears and phobias

- Small spaces
- Elevators
- Being away from parents
- The dark
- Germs
- Scary dreams
- Growing older
- Thunderstorms
- Riding a bike
- Dogs

- Swimming
- Bugs
- Taking tests
- Going to bed
- Clowns
- Public speaking
- A new class
- Planes
- Crowds
- Heights

- Loud noises
- Strangers
- Snakes
- Blood
- Mice
- Making mistakes
- Throwing up
- Man with gun
- Dentists
- Bees

STEP 1: Half-fill the spray bottle with water and add a few drops of glycerin, which will keep the glitter from sinking too quickly to the bottom. Add a few drops of the essential oils—just enough to give off a nice scent without being too overpowering. Add the glitter and top up the bottle with water. Put the lid on and shake it up. This is the special fear-fighting spray.

STEP 2: Give kids this spray and allow them to create a "force field" around themselves whenever they sense anxiety beginning to take over their body. As they use the spray to bounce back those feelings of fear, children learn that they have the power to fight back.

STEP 3: Once the force field has been created, ask them to close their eyes and take one deep breath in and out. Ask them to think about or speak aloud one positive affirmation, quote or thought, such as "I can do this," "I am safe" or "This will not defeat me."

Tools for overcoming fears and phobias

Fear is a natural impulse that instinctively compels us to get out of harm's way to ensure our survival. But when normal fears escalate into irrational phobias, they stop protecting us and can actually cause damage instead. When that happens, the only way to rein them in is to face them head-on.

As parents, we naturally want to protect our children from all forms of suffering, but continually avoiding situations that are not truly dangerous only feeds kids' anxiety. Asking children with anxiety to lean into the cause of their intense distress is a very difficult thing to do, but it's exactly what's needed if they're to control their anxiety rather than letting it control them.

By this point, you've likely tried to tackle these fears before and met with only minimal success. You may be both hesitant to try again and skeptical that anything will actually make a difference. However, gradual exposure to the trigger through a carefully devised plan will desensitize children's fear response, decreasing the overwhelming thoughts and feelings until they reach a point where the trigger no longer produces any anxiety at all.

Keep in mind that this exposure needs to be undertaken with great care; pushing kids too far, too fast will not have positive effects. I encourage you to be patient and hopeful, always putting the attachment between you and your children above the success of the exercise. As kids are facing their fears, they are very vulnerable and will be extra sensitive to your reactions to their successes and setbacks. By encouraging them to persevere and letting them know that it really is okay to feel that fear, you'll soon be pushing back against it together. In doing so, children gain confidence, resiliency and coping strategies, and their whole body system learns new responses to old patterns.

LEVELING UP AND OUT OF FEAR AND PHOBIAS
Good for all ages
Materials needed: game template, task cards, a list of effort rewards
Fighting fear step-by-step takes some creativity if you're going to get kids to *buy in* to facing what they dread the most. To help, we've leveraged children's innate love of games to safely and progressively expose kids to their biggest fears. Framed as a three-level video game, this system allows you to tackle these fears in manageable stages. As with most video games, kids earn rewards as they master each level. As they move through the levels, their capacity increases until they are ready to face the ultimate fear (or boss) head-on and win the game.

STEP 1: Start by explaining the purpose of the exercise so kids are on board with the process and understand they're in control. Let them know that fighting fears is a step-by-step pursuit, just like mastering a video game. Sometimes it comes easily, and at other times it takes persistence. As they progress through the levels, fighting their fears will become more challenging. But remind them that every step prepares them for the next and that they never have to take on more than they can handle. In this game they'll beat three different bosses: Master Worry, Anxiety Invader and The Great Fearful. To defeat each boss, they'll need to master three tasks.

STEP 2: Help kids identify a target fear, making it as specific and measurable as possible. For example, "fear of petting a dog" is more useful than "fear of dogs." Work with them to make a list of the situations that will allow them to gradually but successfully level up to that fear and complete the game. Keep the challenges practical, doable and specific. This could involve breaking tasks down into even smaller steps. For example, the task "watching dogs" might become two steps: first, watching a movie with a dog

Suggested rewards

Create your own list of rewards according to your children's preferences and the resources available. Here are some ideas to get you started:

LEVEL 1 EFFORT REWARDS

1. a comic book
2. watching a movie
3. playing a board game
4. a package of stickers
5. a favorite snack
6. a new book
7. an hour of outside play
8. baking with a parent

LEVEL 2 EFFORT REWARDS

1. going to the pool
2. going ice skating
3. having a sleepover
4. going to a movie
5. going out for lunch
6. riding a bike with a parent
7. ordering pizza for home delivery
8. buying art supplies
9. eating an ice cream
10. going to the water park
11. buying a new poster
12. having a picnic

LEVEL 3 EFFORT REWARDS

1. going camping
2. visiting a local attraction
3. having an all-day picnic at the beach or a park
4. taking a day trip
5. buying new clothing
6. buying a new game

in it, then looking at live dogs at a dog park (safely from the car window).

STEP 3: Once the list of tasks is complete, write them on cards and ask the kids to order them from easiest to most difficult. Use the Leveling Up and Out of Fear template (page 121) to divide the list into three levels.

STEP 4: Create a list of effort rewards. While children generally focus far less on rewards when they start to notice their successes (because feeling better is a strong motivator), these effort rewards can provide extra motivation to remain committed to the plan. It's important to reward effort rather than success—failing to achieve a reward can add punishment to pain. Instead, explain that every time they attempt to defeat a boss, they will receive an effort reward, which can make working towards a goal more fun. Together, think of as many rewards as you can in a variety of sizes to suit all three levels.

STEP 5: Start the game! Before and after each task, encourage kids to check their amygdala meter (page 67). If they feel like they are in a danger zone (yellow or red) at the end of a task, stay at the same level and repeat it again at a later time. Keep in mind that they may need to revisit a task a few times before moving on to the next one. If kids feel they are in the green zone (safe and in control) at the end of a task, let them know that they have "leveled up" and are ready to move on to the next stage. If any of the tasks is especially difficult for them, try to break it down into smaller steps, rewarding each sub-step with encouragement, understanding and an item from your reward list. Always praise children for the hard work they've done, even if they haven't reached the green zone. Facing fears is a difficult process and their engagement in the exercises is something they can be proud of.

Online bonus: More level-up grids

Download your own Leveling Up and Out of Fear Strategy Chart and find detailed and specific steps to help children "level up" out of other common fears at michelekambolis. com/resources.

1. social anxiety
2. spiders
3. injections
4. swimming/water
5. public speaking

Leveling Up and Out of Fear Strategy Chart

LEVEL	FEAR: DOGS	BOSS TO BE DEFEATED	STRATEGIES TO LEVEL UP
LEVEL 1 Things that worry me a little	Seeing a dog from a distance	 Master Worry	1) Watch dogs on TV or YouTube. 2) Go to a pet store and look at the dogs in cages. 3) Go to an on-leash park and look at dogs from a distance. **LEVEL UP!** Level 1 Complete!
LEVEL 2 Things that are difficult for me	Being close to a dog	 Anxiety Invader	4) Go to an on-leash park and move close to a dog. 5) Move a bit closer. 6) Stand next to a dog. **Level UP!** Level 2 Complete!
LEVEL 3 Things that are very difficult for me	Petting a dog	 The Great Fearful	7) Hold a dog's leash. 8) Let a dog smell the back of my hand. 9) Pet a dog. **GAME OVER!** Level 3 complete!

PARENTING TIPS:

1. Assure children that they won't have to take on all of the challenges at once and that you won't ask them to do anything they aren't ready for—you'll go at their pace.

2. Before starting any sort of exposure, give children resiliency/coping tools they can use when they start to feel overloaded, e.g., deep breathing, mindfulness activities, relaxation techniques and thought busters.

3. If kids continue to express resistance, discuss what is creating a roadblock for them. Let them know that they can always change the levels to break things down into even smaller steps, if there is a missing level that needs to be added. The key here is to emphasize flexibility, but full avoidance is not an option. With your support and steady guidance, they won't be going through this alone.

4. Take small steps! Each level should be difficult enough to provoke some anxiety but easy enough that children can have some confidence that they will be able to do it.

5. Keep tasks simple and straightforward to avoid overloading kids. Their brain is going to be using a lot of mental energy in the moments when they are exposed to their fear, and making things too complex may trip them up.

Tools for refocusing anxiety

When children become anxious, even the best calming and thought-busting strategies don't always work. One way to help kids slow down and get a better hold of their anxious thoughts and feelings is to engage in an activity that shifts their focused attention away from the difficult circumstance or thought. The point here is that we can choose where to focus our attention. Refocusing activities should be complex enough to leave little mental energy for the situation that is causing kids the distress.

6. To help children progress to the next level, try as simple a change as the location where they face their fear (e.g., watching a dog in the dog park after watching a dog at the local breeder). This way kids can experience it in different situations and feel safe, which sends a message to their brain system that this is not a stimulus that requires a big reaction.

7. Another way to progress to the next level might also be just to spend a little more time with the fear (e.g., standing next to a dog for ten minutes rather than five).

8. When you incorporate the exposure exercises into children's daily routine, they get regular practice dealing with their fear, so they aren't left feeling caught off guard. If the activities are spaced too far apart, kids don't have the opportunity to develop consistent responses to the fear stimulus and strengthen new pathways in the brain.

9. Keep note of the progress kids are making and generously remind them that "on the other side of fear lies freedom." Be specific about the freedoms they can look forward to (for example, "Once you're done this level, you'll be able to sleep over at your friend's because you'll have conquered your nighttime fear!").

LAST LETTER

Best for ages 8 and up

Materials needed: none

This easy game can be used with older kids. If you know that your kids are going to be in a situation that will be distressing for them, use it preventatively to ensure their anxiety levels don't peak into the red zone. Some kids use this game to redirect their focus from feelings of panic when they're stepping outside their comfort zone while fighting fear.

STEP 1: Begin by choosing a subject category—anything from foods to animals, video games or geographical locations.

STEP 2: Once you've picked a category, have children think of one thing in that category. For example, if the subject is animals, they might say "mouse." The next person must think of another animal whose name begins with the last letter of the first animal; in this example, you might say "elephant."

STEP 3: Continue playing until you're stumped and cannot continue the chain. If this point comes too quickly, you can always start over!

CLICK
Good for all ages
Materials needed: paper and pens or markers
This activity can help to manage children's anxiety temporarily because it requires them to focus intently on a physical object and remember it rather than ruminating on the anxious thought. Because you know your child best, you'll intuitively sense when it's useful for them to quell anxiety by focusing externally and when it's time to observe internally.

STEP 1: Start by explaining that the brain can act like a camera, holding images of what we've seen.

STEP 2: Ask kids to close their eyes, take a deep breath in and let it out. When they open their eyes, have them cup their hands around their eyes and use this "lens" to focus on one specific item in the room. Whatever they choose should be completely unrelated to their fear. Have them gaze at the item for thirty seconds (let them know when it's time to "click" the picture) and then close their eyes again. Ask them to picture that item and all its details in their mind for a moment.

STEP 3: Once they open their eyes, give kids a pen and paper and allow them to draw the item to the best of their ability. While they're drawing, it helps to describe the item out loud and say what they noticed about it.

STEP 4: When the drawing is finished, ask children to close their eyes again, take a deep breath in and then gently let it out to bring them back to full body awareness.

Tools for mindful breathing

In one very famous study, the Framingham Heart Study, researchers followed thousands of people over a thirty-year period. They discovered something groundbreaking: that how well we breathe is the single most important factor in determining overall health, including anxiety levels. Breathing is the only function of the body that we perform both voluntarily and involuntarily. In times of stress, our sympathetic nervous system becomes overstimulated and we might begin to hyperventilate, which can be terrifying for children and adults alike. That involuntary rapid breathing lowers carbon dioxide levels in the body, restricts blood flow to the brain and leads to the symptoms of panic (racing heart, tingling hands or feet, dizziness, feelings of terror, etc.). Breathing mindfully allows us to voluntarily activate the parasympathetic nervous system and calm the body. Just knowing and practicing the simple art of mindful breathing can vastly improve the well-being of children with anxiety. At the very least, it's a big step in the right direction.

When children learn that mindful breathing will help to fend off their fight, flight, freeze or dive response, they're usually eager to give it a try. But its effects aren't always immediate, so it's helpful to remind them that working out with mindful breathing regularly throughout the day will, in time, make its effects more powerful. It's like exercising any muscle; the more you flex it, the stronger it becomes. And kids are fascinated to know that something as simple as deep breathing can slow down their heart rate, lower their blood pressure and release powerful chemicals in the brain that leave them feeling happier overall.

SQUARE BREATHING AND MONKEY MIND
Good for all ages
Materials needed: none
Square breathing is a great solution for children who want a covert way to deal with their discomfort. Many children use square breathing to combat test or performance anxiety: they're able to quietly enjoy the effects of square breathing without anyone noticing.

STEP 1: Have children think about whether they sometimes notice their thoughts racing through their mind or their heart beating fast. Let them know that a racing mind or heart is their body giving them a warning that they may have too much stress. It's that amygdala (page 61) again, and it's like having a wild monkey in their mind that's jumping around and swinging from tree to tree. Monkey Mind can be distracting, and make us irritable or anxious.

STEP 2: Let them know that one way to tame Monkey Mind is to use a special way of breathing called square breathing. Square breathing helps us lower our heart rate and put the monkey to sleep.

STEP 3: Ask them to imagine breathing around a square. Start at the bottom left-hand corner and breathe up the square by inhaling for four counts—one, two, three and four.

STEP 4: Now ask them them to hold their breath along the top of the square while you count—one, two, three, four.

STEP 5: Next have them exhale along the right side of the square while you count—one, two, three and four.

STEP 6: Finally, have them hold their breath again along the bottom of the square: one, two, three and four.

STEP 7: Encourage kids to continue square breathing until they notice their thoughts become more still. Sit for a moment together and enjoy the effects.

PARENTING TIP: Some children find square breathing difficult, but they can easily master triangle breathing: inhaling along one side, exhaling along the second side and holding their breath to finish.

Most children find holding their breath after the exhalation to be the most difficult step. They may have had all kinds of practice holding their breath underwater or in contests to see who can hold their breath the longest, but holding after the exhalation feels new. Teach children that they can avoid taking a sip of air by placing their hand on their tummy; it's the easiest way to track whether or not air is coming in.

BUBBLE BREATHING

Best for ages 4–9

Materials needed: bubble bath, essential oils (optional), bubble soap and wand, drinking straw

As children start to feel more comfortable with belly breathing, try to incorporate it into different parts of the day. Making focused breathing a part of children's routine helps them to become mindful of the sensations in their bodies, so use natural tasks and activities to cue practiced breathing. For example, bubble baths are a fun and enjoyable way for children to relax, let go of their worries and focus on their breathing. Other possible cues to practice belly breathing could be waiting at a traffic light, going to the washroom, driving in the car, walking home, waiting for an elevator and waiting in line at the grocery store.

STEP 1: Run a bubble bath adding essential oils that children find relaxing and soothing.

STEP 2: Give kids a bottle of bubbles and a wand and see the fun begin. Encourage them to breathe in for four counts, making their belly blow up like a bubble, and then gently exhale for four counts, releasing the bubble in their tummy into the wand to blow a big bubble. (Alternatively, give them a straw to create their own bubbles in the water. The idea here is grand mastery of the power of deep breathing.)

STEP 3: As you blow bubbles together, breathe deeply and enjoy the spirit of your intention. It can be helpful to remember that something as simple as taking a moment to breathe, connect and delight in your child will heal their inner wounds. While tools are powerful, our willingness to wholeheartedly value ourselves and our children in the moment matters most.

MINDFUL BREATHING

Good for all ages

Materials needed: none

Master mindful breathing by practicing first in a quiet space. Then practice several times throughout the day by ringing a bell or other calming sound to let the family know it's the perfect time to stop, turn inward, breathe and simply notice for a few minutes.

STEP 1: Have kids create a comfortable, quiet space where you can sit together.

STEP 2: Ask them to scan their body from head to toe, perhaps using their amygdala meter (page 67) to tell you what level of stress they're feeling overall. Then, close your eyes together and listen to the sound of your breath. Encourage children to simply notice their breathing and let their tummy fill up like a balloon. Notice it rise and fall.

STEP 3: As kids notice their thoughts, encourage them to simply label them as "thought." Remind them that as their mind wanders and thoughts come in, they can just come back to noticing their breathing again.

STEP 4: Continue until you notice their attention wandering (expect that young children may only attend for a short time) and ask them to open their eyes and slowly bring their attention back into the room.

STEP 5: Invite kids to check their amygdala meter again and see the difference after their mindful moments.

PARENTING TIP: To get the full benefits of mindful breathing, remember the importance of regular practice. Some children may initially find that relaxing in such a purposeful way feels uncomfortable. Take a few moments afterwards to connect with them and discuss what their experience was like and how they are feeling in the present moment. If they get upset or frustrated with themselves for not being able to focus, let them know that feeling distracted or unable to concentrate is okay and that it happens to everyone, even master yogis. There is no shame in struggle, and the distraction that naturally shows up during mindful breathing is a chance to embrace our imperfection.

Tools for developing mindfulness

Mindfulness is a state of active, open attention on the present. It is now being used increasingly as an integral part of social-emotional learning in classrooms across North America to help kids observe their thoughts and feelings from a distance, without judgment. Mindful breathing is at the heart of this practice and it's an essential tool for children with anxiety, but mindfulness involves much more than breathing. Turning inward and scanning the internal landscape helps children better connect with and accept their thoughts, feelings and body sensations.

MINDFULNESS GLITTER BOTTLE

Best for ages 5–12

Materials needed: Empty water bottle, one tube glitter glue, one tube dry glitter

Observing thoughts can be a tough concept even for adults, let alone young children. Slowing thoughts to a level where kids can see them is made much easier when they have tools to clear away the clutter in their minds. To create your own Mindfulness Glitter

Bottle, first remove the label from an empty water bottle. Fill the bottle ¾ full with hot water and then add a few squeezes of glitter glue and a tube of dry glitter. Screw on the cap and play with the mixture to see how long it takes for the glitter to settle to the bottom. The trick is to play with the ratio so that the glitter settles slowly— add more glitter glue to slow it down and more water to make it settle more quickly. Super glue the cap on once you figure out the right consistency.

STEP 1: Have kids sit with you in a comfortable and quiet area. Give them the glitter bottle and ask them to shake, shake, shake it until the glitter is swirling around like busy thoughts in their brain. It's just like when the amygdala is on high alert and sending out thoughts and sensations that are spreading everywhere.

STEP 2: Take a few deep breaths in and out together, and encourage kids to simply join you in noticing the glitter as it settles to the bottom.

STEP 3: Encourage them to imagine the glitter as thoughts—without worrying about what the thoughts are or what they mean. Kids can simply notice the thought, name it as "thought" as it passes by and watch as it floats around. As the glitter starts to settle, ask them to imagine that the thoughts and ideas in their mind are settling too, gently clearing away the cloud in their mind.

> **PARENTING TIP:** As you watch the glitter settling to the bottom of the bottle together, engage kids in some deep breathing exercises to help them slow down their mind. Their brain and heart will connect your presence with the sensation of relaxation and calm and they will know there is no scarcity to the care you provide.

SPIDEY-SENSES

Good for all ages

Materials needed: paper and pens, magazines or downloaded Internet pictures for collage, blindfold (optional)

Stressed children can lose sight of what's happening around them because of a surge of chemicals in the brain that are elevating their fight, flight, freeze or dive response. When their amygdala (page 61) is triggered, their hippocampus (page 61), which helps to recall memories doesn't work very well and it becomes very difficult for kids to take notice of the things that soothe them. This activity helps them access those past experiences of comfort and enjoyment and trains the brain system to activate the pleasure centers (releasing the feel-good chemicals) in the moment. The more aware kids are of what brings them a sense of well-being, the better able they'll be to access those memories and sensations when their minds are racing. The more they practice, the more quickly and easily they'll be able to shift their thoughts from stress to pleasure. And you may come away with a better sense of the things that bring calm—information you can use to help kids when they need it most.

STEP 1: Let kids know that they have powerful spidey-senses that can help their brain release feel-good chemicals like dopamine. Just thinking about the things we like makes us feel good!

STEP 2: Working together, create a list of four or five things they enjoy smelling. Better yet, have them create a collage of their favorite smells. Some children may choose images of a rose garden, cotton candy, mom's scarf—I've even had a child choose a picture of a bunny. The choices may not always seem logical, but that's okay. Smell powerfully elicits deeply held memories, so the selections may be more emotional than rational.

STEP 3: Make similar lists for the rest of the senses: children should have five lists in total, each with four or five things they enjoy tasting, seeing, hearing, touching or smelling.

STEP 4: Take the mindfulness experience further by collecting some of the items on the lists. Do you feel a surge of happiness as you assemble these items? Make the activity more playful by letting kids blindfold you and hand you an item to see if you can figure out what it is.

5, 4, 3, 2, 1—NOTICE!

Best for ages 5–10

Materials needed: none

This exercise engages children with their present surroundings, which shifts their mental energy away from anxious thoughts and brings their attention to their present surroundings. Doing this activates their awareness and helps them shift from *being in* the storm to *watching* the storm from a safe distance. It reinforces the habit of reflection rather than response, and can help everyone to fully accept the moment they are in—no matter how difficult. The pause can be just what's needed to allow the brain system to quiet down.

STEP 1: Have kids compare what it's like when they're stressed to what it must be like in the eye of a storm. They might be running late for school and can't find their shoes, backpack or homework. When we're in the eye of the storm, all kinds of information just swirls together but we remain mostly calm and focused. Explain that you're going to teach them a way to remain in the eye of the storm, until it passes.

STEP 2: Let kids know that you're going to count down things they can notice using their five senses, starting with their eyes. Ask them to look around and name five different objects in the room. Have them describe what the objects look like: their shape, texture, color, and so on. Notice what their eye is most drawn to and let your natural curiosity lead the way to finding out more. ("What feeling comes up when you look at that? What do you notice most about it?") With young children, you might want to take turns noticing and describing things, to help keep them engaged.

STEP 3: Next, have children notice four things they can *feel* with their hands or body, and describe the experience to you. Ask them to focus on each item as if they are experiencing it for the first time.

STEP 4: Next, have them identify three things they can hear. Experiment by listening with your eyes open and then closed. Notice how closed-eye listening can help quiet the mind, giving us more mental focus.

STEP 5: Share two things you can smell.

STEP 6: Finish up with one thing they can taste.

> **PARENTING TIP:** Smell and taste tend to be the most difficult senses to notice. If kids have difficulty bringing attention to these senses, you can alter the exercise so that they revisit their previous senses. Some children may find it easier to go from describing one object to five, rather than starting with five. Flexibility is the intended spirit of all your playful moments with your child, so let kids take the lead and allow them to make it their own.

HARNESS YOUR SUPER AWARENESS POWER!

Best for ages 6–10

Materials needed: Super Awareness Power template or paper, pens

How often do we actually step back and just observe both our inner and outer experience? If we're honest, many of us wait until after the kids are in bed or, worse, until we're on vacation once a year before we sit and truly reflect. When we learn to notice our feelings, our thoughts and our physical sensations as well as what is going on around us, we access the power of "super awareness"! When this power lies dormant, any one thought or feeling can dominate how we think, feel and act. When we acknowledge our super awareness, we *choose* what we focus on and for how long. Focused awareness engages our prefrontal cortex, which allows us to step back and see the big picture so we can make sense of our reality and make better-informed decisions.

Often we take a thought or a feeling and apply it to our whole selves; for example, we say "I *am* worried" versus "I *feel* worried." By harnessing their super-aware power, children can begin to see the many aspects of their experience and understand that they are not a thought or feeling, they are so much more. Using the exercise daily, at a specific time in the day, helps children see that thoughts, feelings, sensations and environmental experiences do change over time.

STEP 1: Begin by explaining to kids that there is a place inside of us where we store a secret power called Super Awareness that can relieve anxiety, stress and worry. When we draw on our Super Awareness, we have power over our thoughts, feelings and body sensations because we *choose* where to place their focus. This means less worry, more self-compassion and fun! Let children know that you will be doing this exercise with them and that you

Online extra: Super Awareness Power template

Download and print out your very own Super Awareness
Power template from michelekambolis.com/resources.

are also working on worrying less, accepting yourself more, having more fun and being a joy-filled, super-aware adult!

STEP 2: Show kids the Super Awareness Power example sheet. Introduce them to Lisa, the character in the middle of the page. Lisa has the power of Super Awareness! To activate her power, she closes her eyes really, really tight and says "Super Awareness!" Think of a way you'll activate your own power and demonstrate that.

STEP 3: Ask kids how they will activate their Super Awareness. Get them to show you. If they are having trouble thinking of something to do, feel free to help them with ideas.

STEP 4: Using a copy of the Super Awareness template for each person, draw yourselves in the center of the templates as superheroes. If you aren't able to download the template, simply use a blank sheet of paper, copying the arrangement of items in the example sheet.

STEP 5: Using Lisa as an example, go through each of the categories and think of a list of thoughts, feelings and body sensations that you are noticing in the moment. When you list how you feel, make sure you say, "I feel _____" instead of "I am _____." This makes it clear that *you* are not your feeling—your feeling is just one of many parts of you.

STEP 6: Help kids to fill out their sheet. They may initially need some prompting; remember, your prefrontal cortex is much more developed than theirs! Invite children to choose which of those thoughts, feelings and body sensations they would prefer to focus on. With practice, they will find activating their Super Awareness easier.

Tools for visualization

For kids to develop the ability to observe themselves from a distance and awaken to the practice of internal regulation, they first have to become aware of what they're actually experiencing. Imagery and visualization are great ways to tune into our inner world—these tools are like watching our own internal movie, in vivid Technicolor. Once children can follow guided visualization, they're better able to notice and name the sensations in their bodies, the memories that may be clouding the way they're managing situations or relationships, and the feelings that may be affecting their peace of mind. They can then learn to influence these, as well as their intentions and dreams. The following exercises are presented as scripts that can be spoken aloud to kids, or modified as you wish.

WATCHING CLOUDS
Good for all ages

Watching clouds is a great visualization activity just before bedtime because it gives kids a chance to slow down their thinking process, decrease their level of arousal and let go of the thoughts that may interfere with sleep. Taking time out of the day for relaxing visualization has also been shown to help people with anxiety because it decreases their negative thinking patterns and activates the parasympathetic nervous system, which brings calm to the body. Research has shown that the more often we engage in visualization, the better we can shift our thinking to more positive ideas, which makes us happier and improves our overall mental health. Start by inviting children to sit or lie down with you, close their eyes and take in a few gentle deep belly breaths.

Sample script
Let's imagine we are lying somewhere wonderful, staring up at the clouds in the sky. You can decide where; it could be in a field or

on a beach. It's a beautiful sunny day, not too bright though—a perfect day to watch the clouds drift by. These clouds are special: each one has a thought, feeling or idea on it.

Let's take a look at the first cloud drifting by. Notice what's inside and just observe it without thinking too deeply about it, then watch it drift out of sight. Do you see the next cloud? Again, just notice what's inside it and observe it as it gently floats away.

As you watch the clouds, you might notice that a few of the ones floating by are blank, and that's okay. Just watch them gently drift by and right out of sight. If you want, you can think of a positive or relaxing word that you can fill that blank space with; for example, joy, peace or calm. If you can't think of one, that's okay too. Just keep watching those clouds as they slowly and gently drift by in your mind.

THE WORRY BANDIT

Best for ages 5–10

Children love this imagery exercise; it's playful and engages their inner trickster. Start by inviting them to sit or lie down with you, close their eyes and take in a few gentle deep belly breaths.

Sample script

Let's close our eyes and go on a little adventure to see if we can settle down our worries. Start by imagining that you are going about your day, either at home or at school. Suddenly, out of the corner of your eye you see something that you have never seen before. You turn to get a closer look and discover it's the Worry Bandit!

You've heard about the Worry Bandit before, but you have never seen him with your own eyes...until now. He's mischievous and crafty and he likes to help kids in a super-sneaky way. He spends his days roaming around looking for worries to snatch.

What do you think he looks like? He may be short or tall, skinny or plump, have dark or light hair, have a pointy nose or a mustache.

Notice him tiptoeing towards a girl in the playground ... She's sitting on her own, and she's very worried about something! Now that she isn't looking, he quickly tiptoes up behind her and snatches her worry away! She doesn't seem to mind. She must have been ready to let go of it, because the Worry Bandit only steals worries that kids don't want anymore. She looks happier now, and she's smiling a big toothy grin.

It looks like the Worry Bandit has noticed you! Do you have a worry you want to get rid of? If you do, the Worry Bandit will happily take it away! He's always hungry for worries, and the bigger the worry, the more delicious it tastes to him. Try to think of a worry that you don't want anymore, then once you come up with one, think about it really hard ... The Worry Bandit is on his way right now. He's coming to snatch that worry away! As you're thinking, pretend that you don't know he's coming; remember, he likes to be sneaky.

Suddenly you feel a gust of wind, then it's gone. That was the Worry Bandit snatching your worry away. How delicious it was! Notice how you feel now that you no longer have to worry about that thing. Do you feel relieved, calm, happy ... more relaxed? Remember that the Worry Bandit is always hungry. Do you have another worry you want to let go of? Just think about letting it go and let him gobble it up!

THE FOREST VISUALIZATION

Best for ages 7–12

This exercise allows children to quiet their mind by imagining themselves in a safe, secure and serene place. Here, the forest is as an escape from everyday worries and fears where they are able to visualize themselves being calm, cool and collected. This activity can be used in the afternoon to de-stress after a busy day, or anytime your child is feeling anxious and needs to chill out. Some kids are afraid of the forest because it seems like a dark scary place with animals that can be dangerous and places you can get lost; if that's the case for kids you're working with, change up the scenario.

Sample script

We are going to the forest to meet a very wise person who knows how to help children find answers to their questions about life, so think of a question before we begin. Let's start by finding a quiet place, where we can sit or lie down comfortably. Are you ready? Take a few gentle breaths and allow your mind and body to begin to relax.

Now, imagine transporting yourself to a lush, green forest far away, where the air is fresh and cool. You can decide to take your parents with you on this forest walk, or you can go all by yourself... the choice is yours. You are standing on a winding path and beginning a long walk through the forest. You can feel the path beneath your feet; it's a mix of soil, moss and fallen leaves. As you take a deep breath, you notice the smell of the forest around you... and with your first few steps you begin to leave all of your troubles behind. As you look around, you see the sun is filtering through the large, green trees, shining a light onto the path. You can feel the warmth of the sun on your skin, and you follow the rays of sunlight along the mossy path. As you wander farther into the forest, your body relaxes and your mind clears. Your worries are moving farther and farther away with each step that you take.

Listen to the sounds of the forest and notice that there are birds chirping in the trees beside you. Their chirps make beautiful melodies, and you begin to whistle along to their song. As you continue on your journey through the forest, you notice that your muscles are relaxing, becoming loose and free. Your arms swing beside you to the rhythm of your footsteps. Your body feels pleasantly heavy, and your mind is relaxed.

In the distance, you notice a small cottage with smoke rising from the chimney, and as you draw nearer, you can smell the woodsmoke. The small door at the front of the cottage is open, and you wander over to take a peek inside. You hear the fire crackling and feel its warm glow surrounding you. And you notice the shadow of a person against the wall. Who is it?

The person in the cottage is expecting you and turns to greet you with kind eyes. You feel safe and comfortable and welcome. You step inside and move towards this wise person because you have a question to ask, a question to help you on your journey. Ask your question, and notice the answer. This reply may come in words or maybe it's a look of acceptance in the eyes. Now, notice how you feel about the answer you receive.

Now that you have your answer, it's time to leave and find your way back home. As you turn to go, the wise person is smiling, as if to say "I'm so glad you exist" and letting you know that you can come again as often as you wish. You start to walk down through the path of trees, feeling warm and content. And as you notice the sun shining through the trees again, you realize something. That person you just visited was the wise person inside yourself!

When you are ready to leave this calm and peaceful forest, slowly begin to reawaken your body. Wiggle your fingers and toes, and stretch if you want to. Slowly begin to open your eyes and return to wakefulness, feeling alert and relaxed. Remember that you can return to this wonderful forest whenever and with whomever you like. When you do, you can leave all of your worries and troubles behind and find the answers to any new questions you have.

PARENTING TIP: Research suggests that with consistent practice, the brain will begin to connect visualization and the feelings of relaxation that follow from it. This means that, in time, simply thinking about the forest will elicit feelings of relaxation in kids who practice this exercise, regardless of whether the entire script is completed or not. Practicing visualization can be a powerful tool to allow kids to feel safe, secure and relaxed, and to help them cope with whatever challenges the day may pose.

Tools for developing body awareness

Imagery and body awareness exercises can be challenging for children. Their short attention span and desire to be active makes it especially challenging to turn inward and notice the subtle cues that tell us when our body is becoming stressed. Feel free to shorten the exercises if needed; for young children, it's better to practice in short bursts more often than for longer, less frequent periods of time. Children love to change the scripts as they go. Allowing them to be in charge of what comes next helps ensure they're having fun and creatively playing an active part in their own relaxation process. Some kids may prefer to lead *you* through the script first, which gives you a chance to demonstrate that you're ready and willing to try something new. Older kids may want you to create an audio-recorded version so they can follow the exercise on their own. Recording the script into a cellphone can allow them to practice independently whenever they need.

You've probably now discovered that explaining the brain science behind these exercises can go a long way towards helping children buy in to their benefits. Remind them that stress causes our brain to release stress hormones (cortisol) from our adrenal glands. Too much cortisol makes it hard to remember, concentrate and learn. Worse yet, it makes us feel anxious and upset. If our cortisol levels are too high for long periods of time, the hippocampus—the area that stores our memories—can become damaged and our body has a harder time repairing itself. The good news is that there are activities we can do each day to decrease our cortisol levels, improve our learning and feel better.

Tools for progressive relaxation

What we are feeling emotionally initiates a complex response within the body. By making the connection between their mind and body early on, children can learn to cue themselves to change their patterns. Progressive relaxation works best when kids lie down, face up; however, it could also be done while sitting in a chair. Practice in both settings so it's easy to do at school or in the car. Here are three story scripts to lead children of various ages through progressive relaxation.

A TRIP TO THE MAGIC LAND OF CHILL
Best for ages 5–9
Lie on your back and close your eyes. Notice your breathing. In and out, in and out. Now, take a deep breath, filling your belly and sigh it out... Let's do that again: take a deep breath, filling your belly and sigh it out... We are going to take a trip to the Magic Land of Chill, where you can relax and chill out.

To get there, we need to fly. Reach your arms up towards the sky, reaching, reaching up and then slowly lower them back to the ground. You are now hovering in the air! You might notice that your body is becoming more relaxed. Let's try that again. Reach your arms up. Up. Up. And slowly lower them towards the ground again. When they've touched the ground, take a deep breath in. And out. In. And out.

Now that you are hovering in the air, you must steer yourself to the Magic Land of Chill. Press down on the ground with one of your heels. Press down. And relax. Let's do it again with the same heel. Press down, down, down. And relax. Nice work!

Let's steer now with the other heel. Press your heel down on the ground. And relax. Again press down, down... and relax. Nice! Notice the difference between a tense body and a relaxed body.

This time, let's just hover. Go ahead and press down with both heels—press them into the ground, tightening your muscles all the way up your leg to your hip. Press harder, and harder, and relax. Take a deep breath in and let it out.

Wow, you're really steering yourself well! And you're almost there... you can see the Magic Land of Chill in the distance. But now you have to steer with your arms. Press down with one of your hands, press into the ground while tightening up the muscles all the way to your shoulder. Press harder, and harder, and relax. Let's do that again. Press the same hand into the ground while tightening up your muscles. Press harder, and harder, and relax. Take a deep breath in, and let it out... Notice the difference between your steering arm and your other arm. Does one arm feel more relaxed?

Now let's steer with the other side. Press your other hand into the ground, tightening up the muscles all the way along your arm to your shoulder. Press harder, and harder, and relax. And again... Press the same hand into the ground, tightening up your muscles. Press harder, and harder, and relax. Finally... you've done it! Take a deep breath in, and let it out. Breathe in, and out. Feel the difference in your body and mind.

Look! You've arrived at the Magic Land of Chill. Let's land ever so gently. Reach your arms up one more time and slowly lower your hands towards the ground. When your hands reach the ground, take a deep breath in, let it go and smile because you've arrived.

Now that we're here, we want to explore! Head out into the sand. Step right into it. Feel its warmth as your feet sink down. Spread your toes wide to feel the sand between them. Then crinkle them up, wiggling your feet deeper into that warm sand. And relax! Take a breath in, and out. Breathe in. And out. Try it again: spread your toes really wide and crinkle them up. Wiggle your feet deeper and deeper into the warm sand. Relax, feel your toes lose tension. Great work!

Oh boy, look over there! Monkeys are waving at you! And they're making silly faces! Let's go play with them. Make a silly face too—wrinkle your nose, stick your tongue out, scrunch your eyebrows and squish your eyelids together. That's a great face! Those monkeys will love it! Now, relax. Notice how different your face feels when it is tense, and when it is relaxed.

The monkeys are coming closer to see your silly faces. Let's make another silly face. Wrinkle your nose, stick your tongue out, scrunch your eyebrows and squish your eyelids together. Stay like that . . . and relax. That was fun! Take a deep breath in, and let it go. Breathe in, and out.

Look, the monkeys want to play some more. They want to tickle you! Suck your belly in to avoid their tickles. Try to touch your belly button to the floor. Keep sucking in . . . and relax! Let's do that again . . . Suck your belly in, stronger this time. Keep going . . . and let it go. Just feel the tension leaving your belly.

Now, we're going to trick the monkeys by pushing our bellies out. Go ahead and push your belly up to the sky like a balloon. Make your belly very round. Push your belly up and up, and let it go. Take a deep breath in and out . . . Breathe in, and out. Let's do that again! Push your belly to the sky, even rounder this time. Try to make your belly look like a balloon. Keep pushing and then let it go . . . Nice job!

After all this fun, we are getting really thirsty! Let's find a tree with your favorite fruit on it. Now, reach up to grab a piece of that fruit with one of your hands. Reach for that fruit, and once you have it, you can make juice! Now go ahead and squeeze all of the juice out. Keep squeezing it! And let go ... Take a deep breath in and out.

Let's make some more juice! This time use your other hand. Reach for that fruit, and now that you have it, squeeze all the juice out! Keep squeezing ... and let go ... Take a deep breath in and out. Notice all that tension leaving your hands, your arms and your body. Take a sip, and feel all that cool, sweet juice flowing into your body.

We've had a lot of fun in the Magic Land of Chill, but now it's time to head home. So, let's smile at the monkeys and wave good-bye, and let's prepare for our trip back. Again, reach your arms up to the sky, to make sure that you're hovering in the air. And now slowly lower them back down to the ground ... slowly. When they reach the ground, you've arrived home safe and sound. Take a deep breath in, and out. Breathe in, and out. Open your eyes whenever you are ready.

A MISSION TO ZYTOFF PLANET

Best for ages 9–12

Before we start, sit up straight or lie down on your back and get comfortable. Feel your whole body evenly weighted on the chair or the floor, and close your eyes.

Your mission, as Chief Commander, is to neutralize Vorb, the leader of the Zytoff clan, who has been attacking your city. First, you must land your vessel on Zytoff Planet, then you must find Vorb and turn him back into the good leader he used to be. You will face many challenges, so it is important to remain calm and steady.

You can use your body scanner to help you remain in the zone. Slowly, breathe in, and out. The scanner checks the energy levels in your mind and body. Stay still; it's checking your legs now. Relax them. Now relax the muscles in your arms and hands too. Don't forget about your chest and abdomen. The scanner has detected some tension. Breathe in, and out. In and out. Okay, your neurochemicals and body energy levels are stable now. Let's get started!

You are now inside your vessel. Take one of your feet and test the engine. Push your heel down on the floor. Push. Push. And relax. And again, push down with your heel. Push. And relax. Test the engine with your other foot. Push it down on the floor. Push... And relax. Again, push down with your heel. Push. And relax. Great! Notice the difference between tension and relaxation. Now you are ready to go into space!

With both feet, push down on the fuel pedal for five seconds: 5, 4, 3, 2, 1. Feel the tension in your legs. And goooooo—You've blasted into space! Your vessel is steering itself towards Zytoff Planet, and the mission is proceeding as planned. Now you can relax.

Soon you will have landed and it will be time to go in search of Vorb. You will need your skills, strength and powers to overcome his dark side and return him to good. So, let's do another body scan to be sure you're ready. Slowly, breathe in, and out. Let the scanner check in with your legs and arms, your chest and abdomen. And finally let it check in with your mind. Breathe in, and out. In and out. Good. Everything is in working order! You are ready!

Here you are at Zytoff Planet. Careful... the vessel is landing! Tighten up your leg muscles by pushing on the floor. Do the same with your arms. Brace yourself for impact! Push down. Push down. Boom! Boom! You've made contact with the ground. The vessel hasn't stopped yet; keep pushing down on the floor with your legs and arms. Hold on! Boom! You've landed. The first part of your mission is complete. Relax. Breathe in, and out. And breathe in, and out. Relax... Nice!

Now it's time to complete the second part of the mission. Step out of the vessel and look around for signs of Vorb. Look, there are some fresh tracks in the mud! You decide to follow them up the road. You are now one step closer to defeating Vorb. Breathe in, and out. Again, breathe in, and out.

Watch your step! It's a dugout! Quick, grab on to that over-hang! Reach one of your hands up and grab on to the bar. Tightly squeeze the bar so you don't fall. Reach up with your other hand to help you, and squeeze both of your hands tightly around the bar. Keep squeezing. Now, use the overhang to get past the dug-out. You'll need to shuffle your hands across the bar. Squeeze. Relax. Squeeze. Relax. You're almost there.

Shuffling across the overhang is hard work! Notice your face muscles tightening up from all the effort. Try tightening your face muscles even more. Scrunch your face: shut your eyes, tighten your mouth and wrinkle your nose. Now relax! Feel the difference between a tensed face and a relaxed face. Once more, tighten your face muscles: your eyes, mouth and nose. And relax. Noticing the difference between being tense and relaxed can help you recog-nize when you are stressed or in control.

Don't forget about your arms and hands. You've been hang-ing above that dugout for some time now, so let's get you out of there! Squeeze your hands around the bar. And relax. Once more. Squeeze. Squeeze. And relax. Phew! You've made it across with-out falling in. Nice work, Commander! Now take a breath in, and out. Relax those hands. Relax your shoulders . . . arms . . . and face.

Activate your scanner once more for a quick body scan. Check in with your legs and arms, your hands, chest and abdomen. And finally, check in with your mind. Is everything very relaxed? Breathe in, and out. Good! Again, in and out. As you're calming your mind and body, you are lowering your stress levels. This helps you gain greater self-control, and stay on task.

As you swing yourself off the overhang, you land on a path. There are Vorb's tracks in the mud again. You are getting closer. You start running, following the tracks as you go. Lift your knees, one at a time... higher... and higher. Finally you arrive at the bottom of a huge tower. You notice the hustling and bustling of Vorb's clan working away. They are preparing for battle.

Remember your mission: you must defeat Vorb in order to protect your city from invasion. Quickly, you hide in a nearby bush. You observe your surroundings, looking for Vorb. There! Up there! You've spotted Vorb, sitting on top of the tower, giving orders to the clan.

Notice your heavy breathing. This mission has been one challenge after another, and you are feeling agitated by all this commotion. Let's do another quick body scan using the scanner. Check in with your legs and arms. Your hands. Your chest and abdomen. And finally your mind. Breathe in, and out. Breathe in, and out. Great job!

Let's finish this mission off well. You need your Dartinator. Reach your arms and hands over your head. Nice. Grab your Dartinator and bring it in front of your body. You need to neutralize Vorb by firing a rewiring dart, which will rewire Vorb's body and mind, making him into the noble leader he once was and rebooting the whole clan as well. Look around for a place with a good view of Vorb because you'll need to aim well.

You find a spot and stabilize yourself against a tree. Aiming your Dartinator at Vorb's leg, you start to focus. You are focusing so well that all the sound around you vanishes. It is only you and your breath. You notice your heartbeat slowing down. Your breathing is smooth and steady. Breathe in. Hold. And out. Hold. Breathe in. Hold. And out. You must fire between breaths. Breathe in. Hold. Squeeze your hand tight. Fire! Breathe out. Let your hand relax. Do it again. Squeeze your other hand tight. Hold.

Fire! Breathe out. Let your hand relax. Follow the dart . . . Has it hit your target? Has Vorb been hit? [Pause].

Yes! You've done it. Vorb falls off the tower, clutching his leg.

Everything stops around you. The rewiring dart is working. Everyone is quiet. You can still hear the sound of your own breathing. Breathe in, and out. Relax. You're not sure what's going to happen next . . . All of a sudden, a bright blue fluorescent light starts to spread across Zytoff Planet. Things are transforming before your very eyes. You've done it! You've transformed Vorb and restored the clan. Wonderful job, Commander!

Your mission is complete. You can head back to your vessel and come home. Congratulations! You've saved your city from ultimate invasion. Breathe in, and out. Again, breathe in, and out, as your vessel comes back to Earth. Open your eyes slowly. You are now back in the room.

NOODLE AND CARROT STICK

Best for ages 3–5

Young children may not yet be ready for complex progressive relaxation exercises like The Magic Land of Chill, but they can enjoy Noodle and Carrot Stick!

Let's start by lying on the floor and imagining what it feels like to be tense. Think of a food that is very tense and rigid, like a carrot stick! A carrot is tall, straight and stiff; it can't really bend or move about. Let's make our bodies look like a carrot stick, with our arms to our sides and our legs together. Make your body as stiff as can be so that you can't really move your arms or legs very easily.

Now that we have a pretty good idea of what it's like to be tense, let's see what it feels like to be relaxed. When you're relaxed, your body feels flexible and can move about easily. What food can you think of that is flexible, bendy and loose? A floppy cooked noodle!

Show off your floppy noodle body by loosening up your legs and arms, moving and waving them around.

Now that you know how to be tense *and* relaxed, you will be able to notice when your body is tensing up like a carrot stick. When that happens, you can call out "Floppy Noodle" in your head and think about relaxing your body like a noodle. When you relax your body, you're sending a message to your brain that you're safe and calm.

RAISING CHILDREN WHO have the courage to be themselves in the face of anxiety requires our wholehearted commitment to embracing the powerful parenting opportunities we have each day. We may not have control over our children's temperament or genetics and we may not be able to change the culture of "insatiability" and "disconnect" in which we live, but we do have the tools to help children leverage the strengths they have, and teach them resilience in the face of the stress. Each of us is called upon to authentically celebrate who our children are, and trust that we are already enough for them to grow and learn through. The activities I've shared are meant to open further possibility. We can't and shouldn't remove all struggle, as struggle creates opening for learning. But with a life practice of self-awareness tools, we can and should guide our children towards a deep sense of resilience—and hope.

SEVEN

HOW AND WHEN TO SEEK PROFESSIONAL SUPPORT

Parents of children with anxiety often ask themselves: "Does my child really need therapy?" or "Might my child just outgrow it?" While we will readily seek help from our family doctor when our kids are coughing and sniffling, mental health symptoms are far less obvious and, for many parents, making the decision to contact a therapist isn't easy.

One of the first questions I ask parents when we first meet is how they found me. More often than not, they have either struggled to find help because of long waiting lists or they've tried many other forms of treatment without success. It can be hard to know what to do when our children are struggling. Often we start by hoping that our children will outgrow the problem, that it's "a phase." Then we begin to question other parents to see if our kids' peers are wrestling with similar concerns. If we see that our children are struggling more than others their age, we begin to worry, and this is the stage at which we often debate with our partner about how serious the problem really is.

One of us may normalize the behavior while the other may exaggerate it. Both are coping mechanisms, and both are strategies to help us with the same concern: that our children are suffering. Often teachers or school counselors have voiced their concerns, as they may see our kids struggling academically or socially or wrestling with low self-esteem. And we've usually sought help from a family doctor, who may have suggested an assessment at a mental health clinic, a pediatric consultation or a trial of an SSRI (antidepressant) medication. Or, the doctor may not have shared our concerns at all—anxiety can be difficult to accurately assess, even for seasoned professionals.

At this point, we face difficult decisions. We worry about the stigma of a mental health diagnosis, but know we need help as we wonder about the right type of treatment for our kids. We don't know whose advice to trust. And we have no idea how even to begin to decide whether a child clinical therapist, psychologist, psychiatrist or school counselor will take the right approach. After all, for most of us this is new territory. It doesn't help that few parents talk openly about having a child with anxiety, and our sense of urgency mounts as we often find ourselves on long waiting lists trying to navigate a complex healthcare system.

Only two-thirds of children with anxiety disorders get treatment, so in my opinion if you have concerns, it's best to err on the side of caution and get them checked out. To help you plan your course of action, we'll look at how to decide when children's anxiety should be professionally assessed and how to find the right treatment team if you need one. Knowing that you are receiving help from trusted professionals who understand your children's needs can be one of the most important steps in creating a healing environment for the entire family.

Clinical levels of anxiety can be hard to identify, and anxiety manifests itself quite differently in children than it does in adults. Children's anxiety may show up as misbehavior, physical illness or separation anxiety, and it *can* be confused with fears that are a part of normal childhood development. You shouldn't expect to be able to clearly identify whether your children's anxiety has moved from "normal" to "clinical," but after reading this chapter you will have a better idea of where on the spectrum it might fall. As with any problem, the most critical point is to support kids in the full context of their being; in other words, to consider the whole family and the cultural system that surrounds it. In his book *Childhood and Society,* Erik H. Erikson, a pioneer in developmental psychology, aptly summarized this view when he wrote: "Do not mistake a child for his symptom."

Avoid focusing on pathology; the point here is not to label kids but to help you better understand the problem and identify what level of seriousness you are dealing with. Clinicians are looking for clusters of symptoms and patterns of anxious thoughts, feelings and behaviors to better understand which particular type of anxiety a child may have. The name might be helpful, but more important is getting at the underlying reasons that are causing the anxiety and the degree of the behaviors resulting from it. Here we'll talk about clinical levels of anxiety and how to identify them, as well as the ways in which "normal" levels of anxiety differ from "clinical" levels.

How are anxiety disorders assessed?

The Diagnostic and Statistical Manual of Mental Disorders 5 (DSM 5) is the professional bible for mental health clinicians, as it contains descriptions of symptoms and lays out the specific criteria for diagnosing mental health disorders. Although it has been periodically reviewed and revised since it was first published in 1952, the fifth edition, published in 2013, made changes to better characterize symptoms and behaviors of mental health concerns based on the most up-to-date research. The information provided here reflects these current descriptions and diagnostic criteria for anxiety disorders.

The DSM 5 isn't designed as a labeling device insomuch as it's a communication tool to help professionals communicate consistently about a mental health condition. Just as when one doctor informs another that a patient has Type II diabetes, a diagnosis of generalized anxiety disorder communicates a wealth of information about the specific care and attention that may be required. In both cases, the doctor has assessed all of the patient's symptoms, used judgment and experience in comparing them with the known literature (in the DSM 5) and suggested the most probable diagnosis. Think of it this way: there is no body without mind and no mind without body. In properly assessing anxiety, it can only help to address the whole being, ensuring that any physiological factors (e.g., asthma, hypothyroidism, allergies) are ruled out and that every treatment approach is considered.

There are seven types of anxiety disorder in children and youth: Separation Anxiety Disorder, Selective Mutism, Specific Phobia, Social Phobia (also called Social Anxiety Disorder), Panic Disorder, Generalized Anxiety Disorder and Agoraphobia, and they are listed according to the typical age of their onset.

SEPARATION ANXIETY DISORDER (SAD)

Separation anxiety is such a normal part of healthy development that it can easily go unnoticed until the problem is quite serious. The main differences between healthy separation anxiety and SAD are the intensity of the fears, and whether these fears keep kids from engaging in normal activities. Children with SAD may become agitated simply by thinking about being away from us and may complain of sickness to avoid playing with friends or attending school.

Separation anxiety can be exhausting for parents, as we lose the freedom to accomplish even the smallest of tasks—even to go to the washroom on our own! When I see children clinging to their parent's leg in the school hallway, I recall my own son welling up with tears each and every time I hugged him goodbye in the first few months of his first-grade year. While I always took the time to calm him before I left, I'd walk down the hall wanting to burst into tears myself, as my left-brain was telling me he was perfectly safe and well cared for, and my right-brain was telling me I was abandoning him.

In time, my son learned to name his anxiety and even expect it. By being able to articulate his panic, he was able to give his teachers the information they needed to support and guide him through his day, reminding him of his "tools" or giving him a hug. He needed a "go-to" adult who could provide the soothing he relied on, and strengthening my relationship with his teacher helped ensure she was able to provide that when I was not around. Eventually, my son's separation anxiety showed up only after long breaks from school, and while it persisted well into grade school, my son is now a secure and thriving teenager.

While there were many times I feared I wasn't doing enough, or I worried that my son's separation anxiety might develop into more serious and debilitating levels of distress, I learned to take solace in what I knew to be important for his well-being—to trust in my ability to meet his needs. While it wasn't a clear path (parenting never is!), I did my best to create a safe space for him to feel his anxiety without shame, I taught him tools to manage his distress and I managed to build a tribe of supports to guide us both through.

Fact: According to Anxiety BC, approximately 12% of children will suffer from SAD before they reach the age of 18. It has two peaks: between ages 5–9 and ages 12–14.

To determine whether children have acute, short-term separation anxiety or a more serious and persistent anxiety disorder, look for a persistent fear of leaving you or anxiety about harm coming to you or others they are close to. They may worry to such an extent about catastrophic events separating you that they refuse to attend activities they typically look forward to. These worries can also show up as nightmares or as physical symptoms such as stomachaches and fatigue. Although the symptoms often develop in early childhood, they can persist throughout adulthood.

Behaviors associated with "normal" separation anxiety versus separation anxiety disorder (SAD)

"NORMAL" SEPARATION ANXIETY	SEPARATION ANXIETY DISORDER (SAD)
Tantrums or crying when left with a babysitter for the first time	Constant shadowing around the house and significant upset when left alone, even if parents are nearby
Tantrums or crying during the first few days of school, pre-school or kindergarten	Recurring complaints of headaches or stomachaches when parents or caregivers leave for work
Clinginess to parents or caregivers after moving homes or losing a loved one	Refusal to sleep alone and/or insistence on sleeping with one or both parents
Symptoms of anxiety at the beginning of a new school year	Refusal to go to school

Diagnostic criteria for separation anxiety disorder (SAD)

To diagnose separation anxiety disorder, clinicians consider at least three of the following symptoms:

1. Recurring excessive discomfort when anticipating or experiencing separations from home, parents or other important caregivers.
2. Persistent and excessive worry about death, illness or injury of parents or important caregivers.
3. Persistent and excessive worry about being separated from parents due to an extreme event such as being kidnapped, having an accident or becoming ill.

4. Persistent refusal to leave home, go to school or anywhere else because of an intense fear of separation.
5. Persistent and excessive fear about the thought of being left alone or without someone they are attached to.
6. Persistent reluctance or inability to sleep away from home or to go to sleep without being near parents or someone else they are attached to.
7. Recurring nightmares with the common theme of separation.
8. Repeated complaints of physical symptoms (e.g., headaches, stomachaches, nausea, vomiting) when separated from parents.

In addition to the above symptoms:

1. The fear, anxiety or avoidance has lasted at least four weeks.
2. The anxiety causes significant distress and affects social, academic or other areas of development.
3. The anxiety is not caused by another disorder.

REFUSING TO TALK: SELECTIVE MUTISM

Selective mutism is the consistent failure to speak in social situations when spoken to, even though kids may speak in other situations. Most children with selective mutism speak to family members at home, but not always. While the onset of selective mutism is usually before age five, it may go unnoticed until kids enter school, when they have more social interactions and are expected to perform tasks such as reading aloud.

The failure to speak has far-reaching implications, including interfering with achievement at school and with normal social interactions. Imagine how difficult it must be for children to enter the playground unable to make friends, share in ideas and speak their mind.

Madison

When I first met her, eight-year-old Madison hadn't spoken a word in more than two years. Her parents showed me videos of occasions when she had spoken openly, and she seemed so free as she twirled around the room playfully asking her mom to "come dance." In play therapy, however, she responded with shrugs and nods, silent even as she delighted in playing with the playroom's pet hamster. Even Lightning didn't have the power to bridge that gap between silence and speech.

Fact: Roughly 20 to 30% of children with selective mutism have an underlying speech disorder, which heightens their anxiety in situations in which they are expected to speak.

Madison seemed as happy with our long silences as she did with our one-sided discussions, and it was easy to keep her engaged with toys and art. The themes in her play seemed healthy enough; they were not directed by chaos and violence or by rigidity and shutdown, as I so often see in the play of distressed kids. She even used anxiety-reduction tools like mindful breathing and progressive relaxation, but fighting her fear of talking was less successful. Regrettably, despite my search for answers, I never really did get any sense of what might have been causing her selective mutism.

Before we reached the breakthrough I'd hoped for, her family moved to another community. They hoped a change in schools would help, although I advised that continuity and staying the therapeutic course was more clinically sound. I often wonder what happened to her and deeply hope she found her voice.

Behaviors associated with "normal" shyness versus selective mutism

"NORMAL" SHYNESS	SELECTIVE MUTISM
Withdrawal in new social situations and staying close to parents	Refusal to talk at school
Use of short responses with unfamiliar people	Difficulty initiating or responding to non-verbal communication (e.g., nodding or shaking head)
Use primarily of non-verbal signals (e.g., nodding or smiling/ frowning) but may provide verbal answers with encouragement	Highly self-conscious use of verbal communication and only at specific times and/or with specific people

Diagnostic criteria for selective mutism

To diagnose selective mutism, clinicians consider the following criteria:

1. Consistent failure to speak in a social situation where there is an expectation to do so, despite speaking in other situations.
2. Failure to speak that interferes with educational achievements or social communication.
3. Failure to speak that is not due to lack of knowledge or from language deficits.
4. Failure to speak that is not due to a communication disorder.
5. Persistent refusal to speak that lasts at least one month.

BIG BAD FEARS: SPECIFIC PHOBIA

Children with what's called specific phobia are persistently, excessively and unreasonably fearful of, or avoid, certain objects or situations in a way that significantly interferes with their life. Some common phobias include a fear of spiders, rodents, snakes, flying, heights, injections and situations where escape is difficult. Compared with other anxiety disorders, specific phobia is more frequently identified simply because it is more prevalent and hard to miss; it's hard to overlook kids screaming in terror as they face a squirrel on the sidewalk (it really does happen!).

Max

Eleven-year-old Max was referred to me with arachnophobia, a fear of spiders. He was quiet and thoughtful, and yet so mentally distracted by the thought of spiders that he constantly scanned the room looking for evidence of them.

We started by building a repertoire of tools he could draw on to cope when confronted with his powerful negative irrational beliefs and unrelenting fear. He was steadfastly determined to overcome his phobia, and so he committed to a daily practice of progressive relaxation, square breathing and visualization. Soon he was ready for the "exposure" phase of treatment: over the course of many months, Max faced successively more intense representations of his fear. As his self-worth grew, so too did his courage. We started with mental images of spiders and moved on to pictures, videos and even dead spiders, until he was ready to face the real thing.

Fact: Approximately 5% of children ages 7–12 and 16% of adolescents aged 13–17 years old are affected by specific phobia. The average age of onset is between 7 and 11 years old.

His initial response to each stimulus was usually a racing heart and a frantic mind, but as he learned there was a limit to how far his body would overreact, he began to surrender to the wave of emotions and sensations. Soon he was able to consciously replace thoughts of "I can't stand it" and "I'll never get over it" with "This isn't so bad" and "I can do this; it's no big deal." A fear that had started as a nine or ten on the intensity scale dropped over time, until sitting on the sofa with a spider crawling next to him brought a fear response of only two or three.

Just as his treatment was coming to an end, Max announced that he'd rejoined the outdoor education program he'd given up due to his phobia. He'd met his goal: his fear of spiders had become only a mild discomfort that was no longer holding him back from a full and thriving life.

Behaviors associated with a normal fear versus specific phobia

"NORMAL" FEAR	SPECIFIC PHOBIA
Feelings of fear when a parent is driving too fast	Refusal to get into a car for fear of being involved in a crash
Feelings of fear and nervousness when having to give a presentation in front of the class	Repeated refusal to attend school due to fear around giving a presentation
Feelings of fear that a parent will die one day after watching a movie about a character who dies	Refusal to be separated from parents for fear that they'll die during the time apart
Anxiety and fear of failing an exam when unprepared	Extreme anxiety before exams, excessive worrying and consistent blanking out during tests
Anxiety at the doctor's office while the nurse prepares a needle	Repeated refusal to have blood drawn despite doctor's orders

Diagnostic criteria for specific phobia

To diagnose specific phobia, clinicians consider the following criteria:

1. Extreme fear or anxiety towards a specific object or situation (e.g., flying, heights, animals, needles).
2. Exposure to the object or situation nearly always leads to immediate fear or anxiety.

3. Active avoidance of specific objects or situations, even if an encounter is highly unlikely. If it is endured, intense anxiety persists.

4. Fear or anxiety that is out of proportion to the actual danger posed by the object or situation.

5. Persistent fear, anxiety or avoidance that lasts for at least six months.

6. Levels of fear and anxiety or avoidance that impair social, educational and other important areas of functioning.

7. Fears that are not better explained by another disorder.

BEYOND SHYNESS: SOCIAL PHOBIA

Social phobias (also known as social anxiety disorder) are extreme feelings of shyness and self-consciousness that build into a powerful and overwhelming fear. It's not unusual for children and youth to feel self-conscious, especially as they enter the tween and teen years. Social phobias often emerge during puberty when changes in the brain lead to an increase in abstract thinking ability. Suddenly children who were previously comfortable speaking freely in front of the class become highly aware that others are watching them. Their fear of appearing foolish may cause them to close off socially and rob them of the ability to go to school, attend social events and make meaningful connections.

Fact: Social phobia is one of the most common anxiety disorders and is experienced by between 8 and 13% of children. The average age of onset is 13.

Look for discomfort in everyday social situations, like at a dance class or a birthday party. If kids seem to get embarrassed easily, avoid social activities, public speaking and group activity in general, it's important to take a closer look.

Behaviors associated with "normal" social anxiety versus social phobia

NORMAL SOCIAL ANXIETY	SOCIAL PHOBIA
Nervousness and performance anxiety before appearing in a school play	Persistent complaints of stomach-ache before school field trips and avoidance of all after-school activities
Worry about giving a presenta-tion at school when unprepared	Ongoing avoidance of school and classes for fear of messing up or saying something wrong
Worry about starting at a new school without friends	Refusal to participate in group activities for fear of being judged or doing something "stupid"

Diagnostic criteria for social phobia

To diagnose social phobia, clinicians consider the following criteria:

1. Extreme anxiety related to one or more social situations, including interacting socially, being observed, performing in front of a group, giving a speech, having a conversation, meeting unfamiliar people, etc., in which others may pass judgment.
2. Fear of being humiliated or embarrassed in a social situation and being judged for acting strangely or showing symptoms of anxiety.
3. Exposure to social situations almost always leads to fear or anxiety.
4. Attempts to endure social situations that lead to intense fear or anxiety or concerted avoidance of social situations altogether.
5. Feelings of fear and anxiety that are out of proportion to the actual threat or danger in the social situation.

6. Persistent fear, anxiety or avoidance that lasts for six months or more.
7. Levels of fear and anxiety or avoidance that impair social, educational and other important areas of functioning.
8. Fear that is not caused by a medication or substance.
9. Fear that is not better explained by another disorder.
10. Fear, anxiety or avoidance that is clearly unrelated to another medical condition.

TERROR TIME: PANIC DISORDER

Panic disorder is a fear of unexpected and repeated panic attacks. It's rare in younger children but may show up as uncontrollable crying, dizziness and feelings of being out of control. Children with early onset panic attacks may have difficulty describing what's happening in their body, and their panic may lead to symptoms of separation anxiety. The attacks are a sudden surge of terrifying physical symptoms, including racing heart, tingling sensations, sweatiness and racing thoughts. These attacks feel so frightening that people who have them often feel they're "going crazy" or dying.

Fact: Just 0.4% of children under the age of 14 meet the criteria for panic disorder. There is a gradual increase in adolescence, particularly in young girls; however, onset tends to occur in the later teen years, ages 17–19. Roughly 15 to 30% of individuals who have panic disorder also have social phobia.

As parents, it can be tempting to step in and help kids overcome that difficult moment. We might try to calm or console our children with advice and soothing words; however, there may be times that even with these calming words, their panic escalates. Although these words are sincere and coming from a place of good intention, they could be leaving children feeling frustrated and even more anxious (see What not to say, below).

Behaviors associated with "normal" nervousness versus panic disorder

"NORMAL" NERVOUSNESS	PANIC DISORDER
Episodic but manageable worry before a test	Chronic episodes of racing thoughts about school performance, pounding heart, terror before a big test
Worry about trying a new sport or activity that can be defused by other thoughts	Panic at the thought of trying something new and refusal to participate
Slight reluctance to leave home and go to new places, which can be overcome with encouragement	Extreme resistance to leave home combined with an unwavering belief that panic attacks are imminent and a decline in the number of perceived "safe" places and activities
Worry and nervousness about making a good impression when meeting a new group of friends that soon settles down	Terror of having a panic attack and passing out in front of friends, feelings of nausea, near silence when in a crowd

Diagnostic criteria for panic disorder

To diagnose panic disorder, clinicians consider recurring and unexpected panic attacks resulting in an immediate and abrupt increase of overwhelming fear and discomfort with at least four of the following symptoms occurring during the panic attack:

1. Palpitations, pounding heart or accelerated heart rate
2. Sweating
3. Trembling or shaking
4. Sensations of shortness of breath or smothering
5. Feelings of choking
6. Chest pain or discomfort
7. Nausea or abdominal distress
8. Feelings of dizziness, unsteadiness, lightheadedness or faintness
9. Chills or heat sensations

10. Numbness or tingling sensations
11. Feelings of being outside the body or that things are not real
12. Fear of losing control or "going crazy"
13. Fear of dying

In addition to the symptoms above, the child experiences one (or both) of the following one month (or more) after the panic attack:

1. Concern and worry about having another panic attack or experiencing the symptoms of a panic attack (e.g., losing control, racing heart).
2. Marked change in behavior that interferes with everyday functioning.
3. Fear that is not caused by a medication or substance.
4. Symptoms that are not better explained by another disorder.

What not to say

A panic attack sends adrenaline pulsing through the body as the brain tries to ascertain whether or not it is in danger and decides on the next response. Being in such a high state of arousal is difficult for anyone and can be quite a terrifying experience for children. There are times when no words can quell a panic attack, but there are some statements that are more likely to help our children feel validated in their experience and safe in our care. And while our state of being may affect the outcome as much as what we say, having a script can be calming when panic attacks.

Avoid saying: "Just calm down, everything is okay."
Telling children to "just calm down" minimizes their feelings in the moment and takes away from just how difficult a task calming down can be. De-escalating a panic attack can be especially difficult for kids who haven't really had a chance to build up tools and strategies to help them decrease their anxiety level.

Instead, say: "This is anxiety. Your body is having a big reaction that's telling you you're in danger when you're not. We can take deep breaths together to settle down your brain and body."

Avoid saying: "Don't worry; it's not that bad."
It can be very frustrating for children with anxiety to be told there is nothing wrong, because for them the panic is all too scary and real. The symptoms they are experiencing are telling them something is very wrong, and it can be even more upsetting to hear that no one else can see that. Knowing how to validate the panicky feeling without overemphasizing the anxiety can be a tricky balance.

Instead, say: "I know this feeling is really scary. You're safe. That panicky feeling won't last; it always has a beginning, a middle and an end. Let's track it by rating it from zero to ten . . . Where is it at right now?"

Avoid saying: "You need to calm down. I'm going to leave you alone for a minute and we can talk when you can pull yourself together."
Feelings of being overwhelmed do sometimes mean that people need some space; however, children in the middle of a panic attack do not want to be left alone. They don't know why they are so scared or what is happening to their body, and leaving them alone can escalate their symptoms, sending the message to their brain that things are getting worse and they need to be on even higher alert.

Instead, say: "I am here for you, and I will help you through this. Moving your body can help, so let's start by lifting our arms up and down."

Avoid saying: "You're just overreacting."
Teaching children the difference between a small problem and a big problem and the appropriate reaction for each is important,

but it really isn't a lesson that is going to stick when they're in the middle of a panic attack. Worse yet, it can reinforce feelings of shame at their inability to change their reaction. Save that discussion for afterwards, when helping them to build a set of tools and coping skills to manage their anxiety and panic attacks.

Instead, say: "You're really upset about what happened. Let's first help your body and brain calm down. There's lots of time to figure out a solution."

Avoid saying: "Just think about something else if you're feeling worried."

When children are in the middle of a panic attack, they are not thinking clearly, so it can be next to impossible to try to switch their thought processes in that moment. Instead, orient them towards their senses: asking children to name what they see, hear, taste, feel and smell can help them to find whole-body awareness and soothe the anxiety response.

Instead, say: "We've prepared for this together and have the tools that can help. Let's start by naming everything we see..."

Fact: The prevalence of agoraphobia in the general population ranges from 0.4 to 1.7%, and its onset in childhood is incredibly rare. The average age for onset is 17.

HOME BOUND: AGORAPHOBIA

Children with agoraphobia are fearful and anxious about leaving home or being home alone. While agoraphobia is rare in children, it is important to be fully informed, since children who are generally more anxious are at higher risk. As well, reports from the University of British Columbia Psychology Clinic show that more than 95 percent of people with agoraphobia also suffer from panic disorder—their world becomes smaller as they try to avoid ever more causes of another panic attack. Given the high correlation between agoraphobia and panic disorder, treating the latter quickly is an important step towards preventing the former.

Parents of children with agoraphobia often find just getting to the treatment specialist the most frustrating step. In extreme cases, it may be possible to find a therapist who will begin treatment with home-based sessions.

Behavior associated with "normal" nervousness versus agoraphobia

"NORMAL" NERVOUSNESS	AGORAPHOBIA
Desire to skip a birthday party because of nervousness in facing a friend after an argument	Feelings of foreboding that intensify to feelings of panic when pushed, despite a desire to join friends
Preference for 1:1 conversation and solitary pastimes like drawing or reading but will converse briefly with others	Eagerness to talk with company at home but refusal to participate in after-school activities and extreme fear and anxiety about visiting others and accepting invitations
Worry about not meeting homework deadlines and nervousness facing parents or teachers to ask for days off or deadline extensions	Avoidance of school for fear of developing panic symptoms and concern about academics because of missing so much school and feeling that it is impossible to catch up

Diagnostic criteria for agoraphobia

To diagnose agoraphobia, clinicians consider:

1. Substantial anxiety about two (or more) of the five following situations:
    a. Use of public transportation (e.g., buses, trains, planes)
    b. Being in open spaces (e.g., parking lots, markets, bridges)
    c. Being in enclosed spaces (e.g., shops, theaters, cinemas)
    d. Standing in line or being in a crowd
    e. Being outside of home alone

2. Avoidance of these situations for fear of being unable to escape or being in danger without available help.

3. Virtually universal feelings of extreme anxiety and fear.

4. Active avoidance of situations that provoke feelings of anxiety or determination to endure them leads to significant distress.

5. Feelings of fear and anxiety that are out of proportion to the likelihood of the danger.

6. Fear or anxiety that is persistent and lasts for six months or more.

7. Fear or anxiety that causes significant impairment in social, academic and other important areas of functioning.

8. Fear or anxiety that is completely unrelated to other medical conditions.

9. Fear or anxiety that is not better explained by a different mental disorder.

Fact: Children usually develop generalized anxiety disorder at about age 12; however, about 3% of children display signs of excessive worry in early childhood and as many as 10.8% in adolescence. From early adolescence on, girls outnumber boys with this condition about two to one, and children with medical issues like diabetes and high blood pressure are at higher risk for GAD.

WHEN THE WORRYING NEVER STOPS: GENERALIZED ANXIETY DISORDER (GAD)

Children with generalized anxiety disorder (GAD) have non-stop and uncontrollable worry about all kinds of topics, from school, friends, health and crime to their parent's job security, natural disasters, death and pets. They often ask a lot of questions to reassure or prepare themselves for a world that, to them, feels like an extra-scary place. Parents of children with GAD may find themselves excessively reassuring and overly preparing children for new experiences, and it's not uncommon for these kids to be extra sensitive to topics in the media, sometimes ruminating about them for weeks at a time.

The worries associated with GAD can be so random that it's often exasperating for parents trying to soothe their kids. Just when one worry has been calmed, another shows up, and the tools used to combat one concern don't always transfer to another. Be on the lookout for perfectionism, self-criticism and a compulsive need to be on time. Also be aware that some children with GAD may appear to be older than they are, ultra responsible and aware of concerns that elude other children their age. It can be challenging to help others understand that this level of conscientiousness is actually problematic perfectionism and should not be reinforced with praise.

Behaviors associated with "normal" anxiety versus generalized anxiety disorder (GAD)

"NORMAL" ANXIETY	GENERALIZED ANXIETY DISORDER (GAD)
Worry about getting sick before an important test when feeling slightly under the weather	Constant worry about school performance while immediately assuming the worst
Nervousness about an important role in a family function (e.g., a wedding) that passes once the role is complete	Heightened anxiety at any special occasion or family event
Worry about loved ones becoming sick after learning of someone they know who has been diagnosed with cancer	Frequent distress about the possibility of natural disasters despite living in an area where no such event has ever occurred
Worry that doesn't get in the way of daily activities and routine	Preoccupation with minute details of appearance and fear that others are internally criticizing them or aware of their anxiety

Ability to control or move on from worry	Worry that is uncontrollable
Worry that, while uncomfortable, doesn't cause significant distress	Worry that significantly disrupts social development or the ability to manage at school
Worry that is limited to a specific, small number of developmentally typical concerns	Worry that varies across many concerns with a tendency to expect the worst
Worry that lasts for only a short time	Persistent worry that is extremely upsetting and stressful

Diagnostic criteria for generalized anxiety disorder (GAD)
To diagnose generalized anxiety disorder, clinicians consider:

1. Constant and intense anxiety or worry related to a wide variety of objects and situations experienced almost daily for at least six months.
2. Little to no control over the worry.
3. In addition to the anxiety, one (or more) of the following symptoms are present:
    ▸ restlessness or a feeling of being on edge
    ▸ fatigue
    ▸ difficulty focusing and concentrating
    ▸ irritability
    ▸ muscle tension
    ▸ difficulty falling or staying asleep
4. Anxiety or fear that leads to marked impairment in social, academic and other important areas of functioning.
5. Anxiety or fear that is not explained by any current medication or a medical condition.
6. Anxiety or fear that is not better explained by a different mental disorder.

The ABCs of therapy: thriving in treatment

As parents, we may be experts about our children, but most of us are not specialists in mental health conditions, which is why treatment for serious clinical levels of anxiety should be guided by a mental health professional. However, parents do play a critical role in kids' recovery and success. The work we do to better understand our own reactions and teach our children the tools to prevent the symptoms that contribute to specific phobia, panic disorder, separation anxiety disorder (SAD) or other clinical levels of anxiety disorder is a powerful first step. The play-based CBT activities will further help children to better regulate their body, calm their neurological system and integrate and influence the messages being sent back and forth between their body and their brain—all important factors in keeping more serious levels of anxiety at bay.

While the symptoms and disorders themselves may sound scary, arming ourselves with this critical information means that we'll be more able to identify a predisposition to any of these disorders, should the need arise. The sooner an anxiety disorder is treated, the better the response. With the right approach, more than 85 percent of children recover.

FINDING THE RIGHT TREATMENT TRIBE

Whether children have a milder form of anxiety or more serious clinical levels, choosing the right therapist is a leap of faith that can be easier when equipped with the right questions. And while qualifications are important, finding the right match is as much based on rapport as it is on credentials.

Asking a family doctor or pediatrician for a recommendation is a great place to start. When these health care professionals know us well, they can better consider which of their colleagues might have the best working relationship with our family. Other people to ask include school counselors, other parents or members of our spiritual community. Local mental health providers or licensing bodies can also provide a list of psychologists or clinical therapists, including information on their areas of specialization.

I always recommend meeting with two or three mental health professionals before making a decision. You may feel relieved after meeting with the first therapist and be eager to get started right away, but your feelings may change after getting a feel for how others work.

Full disclosure, red tape and the right credentials

Many therapists will offer a professional disclosure statement that lists their qualifications, experience and nature of approach. If not, ask what their credentials are. Professional licensing bodies will also have a list of therapists who are licensed to practice in each region.

As a general rule, child therapists should hold a professional mental health degree; psychiatrists, psychologists, clinical counselors and some social workers are also qualified to diagnose and treat mental health disorders.

Psychiatrists (MDs or DOs) are medical doctors with advanced training and experience in mental health assessment, treatment approaches and pharmacology. They are the only professionals, other than other medical doctors, who can prescribe medications.

Clinical psychologists (PhDs, PsyDs, or EdDs) are therapists with a doctorate degree that includes advanced training in the assessment and treatment of mental health disorders. Look for someone who specializes in treating children and teens and their families. Psychologists cannot prescribe medication but are qualified to help clients with medication management.

Registered clinical counselors (RCCs) are therapists with a master's degree in counseling psychology (MACP or MSCP). They are trained in the assessment and treatment of mental health concerns and are licensed in the province or state where they practice. They may specialize in a wide variety of approaches, including clinical or educational psychology, pastoral counseling, child and youth care, marital and family counseling, clinical social work, psychiatric nursing or applied behavioral sciences. They may be qualified to help manage medications, but this varies from one professional to the next. Registered clinical counselors cannot prescribe medication.

Clinical social workers (MSWs or DSWs) are therapists with a master's or doctorate degree in social work, with a specialization in clinical experience. They must have undergone a supervised clinical practicum for at least two years. Clinical social workers focus on the prevention, diagnosis and treatment of mental health disorders, but are not qualified to prescribe medications. They often work in hospitals, community mental health centers or private practice.

When meeting with a psychiatrist, psychologist, registered clinical counselor or clinical social worker, asking some key initial questions can help choose the right professional:

▸ Is the therapist taking new clients?
▸ If there's a waiting list, how long is it?
▸ If the therapist is available, is there a consistent time slot open?
▸ Will the therapist meet for an initial consultation?
▸ If so, is the consultation free?
▸ What type of experience does the therapist have?
▸ Does it include any specific training in working with children?
▸ Does it include a particular approach to helping children with anxiety?
▸ How long has the therapist been practicing?
▸ What types of therapy does the therapist specialize in?

▸ Does it include evidence-based approaches, like CBT, first?

▸ How are parents included in the process?

▸ What qualifications does the therapist have?

▸ Do they include assessing clinical levels of anxiety?

▸ Do they include making recommendations towards or monitoring medications?

▸ Are the therapist's services covered by your health insurance plan's mental health benefits? (If so, ask your policy provider about your plan's yearly budget for mental health services.)

▸ What is the cancellation policy for appointments?

▸ Is the therapist available by phone during an emergency?

▸ If the therapist is on vacation or ill, who is available if needed?

▸ How does the therapist manage confidentiality between children and their parents?

When looking specifically for a play therapist, it can be helpful to ask these additional questions:

▸ Does the therapist have specialized training and supervision in play-based CBT therapy?

▸ Has the therapist earned the credentials of Registered Play Therapist (RPT) or Registered Play Therapy Supervisor (RPTS) issued by the Association for Play Therapy or Play Therapy International?

Why play in CBT therapy?

Most child therapists will have some formal training in play therapy, which builds on children's natural playful instincts and uses them to help kids work through emotional barriers. Play is the natural language of children and it directly honors the spirit of a child's essence. When therapists enter children's world through the language of play, a safe and protected connection quickly grows, giving fertile ground for guiding and repair.

For children aged three to eleven, play therapy is the most widely used form of counseling. Because children develop cognitive skills before language skills, play is the most effective way for them to communicate with the therapist, from deep within their unconscious. The therapist may observe a child playing with toys such as playhouses and dolls, and use art as a way to better understand a child's behavior and assess the problem.

While play lays the foundation for creating the relationship necessary for therapy to be successful, play therapy without more structured CBT activities simply isn't enough for children caught in the clutches of anxiety. Not all play therapists have training in CBT, and not all CBT therapists have training in play therapy; however, if a therapist does have both, it's a powerful child-centered combination.

What happens in play-based CBT?

Play therapists will initially meet with parents to find out about current concerns, gather a child's developmental and family history, and discuss possible approaches to solving the problem. Children then attend three to five therapy sessions to give the therapist time to assess the best course of treatment.

Usually therapists meet regularly with parents to monitor progress, discuss the major themes and concerns, share skills and tools a child is learning and offer suggestions on how to provide support at home.

During a therapy session, children are invited to play freely with puppets, dolls, sand trays, art supplies and other materials that help them express their thoughts and emotions. Older children often overlook the toys and opt to engage with games and art. Not all child therapists work exactly the same way; however, generally they will use a combination of methods to systematically help children address the thoughts, feelings and experiences that contribute to their distress.

Non-directive play therapy allows children to take the lead while a therapist tracks and follows the emotional tone and the stories behind kids' play narratives. Then, during periods of directive play therapy, a therapist takes the lead, introducing and teaching more specific skills and tools, such as strategies for reducing anxiety or changing the mindset or for facing fears step by step—whatever specific tools are needed to meet each child's particular needs. After a few sessions, many child therapists will recommend follow-up activities to do at home; if not, it is worth asking for a meeting to talk about how best to provide this support.

Parents and therapists: partners in successful treatment

I've met with parents who have had both positive and negative experiences with various mental health professionals, and the differentiating factor seems to be how much heart and effort a professional commits to truly getting to know a child.

Therapists who are willing to take the time to get to know a child before giving a diagnosis and who speak with others in that child's life (teachers, parents, other caregivers, etc.) leave parents with a greater sense of confidence in their commitment to the child—and that goes a long way. By giving therapists access to others in our children's life as well as to previous professional assessments, we ensure they have the best, most complete information with which to understand and treat our child to the best of their ability.

Whether children are distressed due to a dynamic within the family or not, studies show that children and families heal faster when parents are involved in the therapy process. At the same time, therapists who work with children and adolescents have the difficult task of protecting the minor's right to privacy while respecting the parent's or guardian's right to information. Privacy is especially important in securing and maintaining the trust necessary for therapy to be effective. Parents can naturally feel uncomfortable or even threatened by it. Know, however, that therapy should never exclude parents, and the therapeutic alliance is not designed to interfere with the deepening of our own parent-child attachment bond. If ever you sense the line between confidentiality and inclusiveness is being blurred, don't hesitate to quickly address your concerns.

In contrast, it can be tempting to hand over responsibility for our children to the therapist or to just switch off (after all, parenting a child with anxiety can be exhausting). While we instinctively know there is no greater gift than our steady involvement, maintaining emotional stamina can naturally be a challenge. It may help to know that children whose parents help facilitate their CBT treatment (either during sessions or through home-based support) are three times more likely to recover, according to research from the University of Reading.

In some cases, therapists recommend an approach called *filial therapy,* in which parents take on the role of therapist and are taught, with the guidance and coaching of the clinician, how to conduct the session. This approach not only secures attachment but bolsters active and empathic listening skills. Whatever the degree of family involvement, our role is integral to our children's healing process.

How to explain treatment to children

"Why do I need therapy?" It's a question many parents hear once children learn they'll be seeing a health care professional. Explaining therapy to kids is actually a lot easier than you might think. Unlike adults, most children are not aware of the perceived stigma of seeing a therapist. While individual therapists may have their own recommended guidelines for explaining therapy, here's a step-by-step guide you might choose to follow:

Acknowledge: Start by letting children know you have noticed they are working really hard at the mindful awareness, belly breathing, thought-busting and fear-fighting activities they are doing and that they are learning some great ways to keep a calm body and mind.

Ask: Check in with kids. You might ask, "Have you noticed a difference since we've been practicing all of the tools together?"

Reflect: Let children know that you've heard their thoughts. You could say, "It sounds like you think that it's helping" or "It sounds like you don't think the thought busters have made enough of a difference. Is that right?"

Inform: Explain to kids who they might be meeting and why while assuring them that you'll be there to support them. You might introduce the idea this way: "We're learning a lot about anxiety and how the brain works, but I want to make sure we're doing everything possible to make sure you feel your most resilient, happy self. So I've met with a special kind of helper for kids called a child therapist. Child therapists help kids work through all kinds of worries and problems."

Describe: Let them know what to expect: "When you meet with the child therapist, you'll see lots of toys, games and art supplies. The therapist will want to get to know you, play, ask questions about what you think and feel and try to understand the things that bother you most. And the therapist will also have lots of suggestions about how to solve any problems that might be coming up—especially stress and anxiety."

Clarify: Set the boundaries, by explaining: "Whatever you talk with the therapist about stays in the 'zone of privacy.' That means the therapist won't tell me, your teacher or anyone else, unless you give your permission. But when you're with the therapist, you can always share whatever you feel like talking about—what you're thinking or feeling or what you did between sessions or a great idea you had. It's like a one-way privacy: the therapist has to keep what you say private, but you don't have to."

Explain: Let children know how you'll be involved. You might say, "I'm going to meet with the child therapist from time to time and sometimes we might even work with the therapist together. That way we can practice at home the kinds of things you are working on with the therapist. It's like doing 'fun work' instead of home-work. After all, I'll be learning too!"

Reassure: And be sure they know they won't be abandoned: "I'll stay in the therapist's office the entire time. If you need me, I'll be right in the waiting room."

How long does play therapy take?

The duration of play therapy varies depending on how severe the problem is and how long the difficulties have existed. However, research suggests that an average of twenty sessions is usually enough to resolve moderate difficulty. Depending on the kids' age, a play therapy session usually lasts about fifty minutes, and weekly sessions are often recommended for optimum results.

EIGHT

OVERCOMING SETBACKS AND OBSTACLES

Anxiety is an essential and important part of life and learning, but it must be monitored and managed or the scale of well-being tips towards distress. Too little anxiety, and kids lack the alarm bells necessary to react to danger or to simply get things done; too much, and they are "worried sick." It can be difficult to find that tender balance between helping children accept their discomfort and taking action towards regulating it, and a few setbacks are inevitable. These changes you're making together may at times call for an inordinate amount of patience. Here, we'll look at ways to bolster our own tenacity and sharpen our skills when hitting hurdles or feeling as if we're at our wit's end.

Setting realistic expectations

Parents often describe to me their internal struggle to try to sort out reasonable expectations for children fraught with anxiety. It's sometimes hard to know where support ends and enabling begins, and this uncertainty can lead to frustration. I'm convinced that by honoring who our children are, we can come to understand what's appropriate and manageable for them. All kinds of charts, studies and infographics describe what children should be doing at what age, but it's essential to set expectations based on what *we* know about *our* children.

We all know how competitive parenting can be. Inevitably, conversations at the playground lead to comparisons of what level our children are at in soccer or reading, how many languages they're learning or how many play dates they have scheduled. While keeping an eye on developmental norms is sensible, measuring success based on the super-child next door (at least according to their parents) only works against our efforts and undermines our confidence about our own kids. With so many Type A moms and dads and their kids against whom to compare ourselves, it can be difficult to dare to parent on our own terms.

All children need room to be fully who they are, with both strengths and vulnerabilities. Those particular strengths and difficulties will vary according to genetics, personality, parenting, home life, support systems and more. Keeping in mind the big picture can help guide our decisions about what may or may not be reasonable for our kids. For example, when we share custody and children are regularly moving from one home to another, they may find it difficult to keep their belongings organized and their schedules on course. Similarly, if we've been burdened with extra projects at work and are pulling longer hours, the lack of time to nurture our parent-child connection can raise their anxiety levels.

I've learned to accept that life is never a straight line. There will always be unanticipated hurdles and it won't always be possible to minimize their disruptive effect; however, there are also some predictable areas that will almost certainly raise stress and anxiety. By anticipating and preparing for them, we can better support our children and reduce both our own anxiety and theirs. For example, symptoms that seemed to have been resolved may reappear. When this happens, it can be easy to assume that children are "getting worse"; in fact, they may be growing into a new level of maturity or learning to master a new challenge. Internal struggle can also go hand in hand with *new* developmental challenges, and remembering that this is natural can provide the motivation to carry on supporting them with confidence whether the hurdle was foreseeable or not.

DEVELOPMENTAL STRESS POINTS

At certain times in their life, all children go through big developmental shifts that cause a surge in emotional and physical discomfort. When my children were in their baby and toddler years, I remember sudden increases in crankiness when they would abruptly be much harder to soothe, lose their appetite or wake frequently in the night. I'd wonder what could possibly be "wrong." However, almost always their internal disruption fell on the heels of a major milestone, like learning to walk or suddenly speaking a surprising number of new words. Children struggling with anxiety seem to feel these stress points even more than other kids.

Take reassurance from the knowledge that the apparent "relapse" is actually a sign of their ongoing growth. Erik Erikson, the forefather of psychosocial development theory, or the stages through which a healthy person passes, explained that children's experience of conflict serves as a turning point in development. Erikson identified eight stages of development (see below), each with a different stress point, or psychosocial crisis, in which an individual's needs come into conflict with society's needs. His belief was that these stress points all carry the possibility of crisis as well as opportunity. In other words, expect setbacks with optimism. Adolescence, puberty, high school exams, early relationships, career choices and leaving home may bring with them a stirring of the anxiety that was all too familiar in childhood; however, with realistic expectations, a strong

Fact: With proper treatment, 85% of children with clinical levels of anxiety overcome it.

parent-child connection to lean on and some experience with emotional mastery, children become better equipped to handle each new phase in life.

Erikson's Eight Stages of Development

STAGE	PSYCHOSOCIAL CRISIS	BASIC VIRTUE	AGE
1	**Trust vs. mistrust** The ability to develop a deep trust that the world is safe and predictable.	Hope	0–1½ years
2	**Autonomy vs. shame** The ability to become independent without a loss of self-esteem due to punishment.	Will	1½–3 years
3	**Initiative vs. guilt** The ability to develop a sense of initiative and security, lead others and make decisions	Purpose	3–5 years
4	**Industry vs. inferiority** The ability to foster approval by demonstrating specific competencies that are valued by society.	Competency	5–12 years
5	**Ego identity vs. role confusion** The ability to learn the roles of adult responsibility.	Fidelity	12–18 years
6	**Intimacy vs. isolation** The ability to forge relationships that lead to long-term commitments with someone other than a family member.	Love	18–40 years
7	**Generativity vs. stagnation** The ability to grow through giving back to society, through raising children, being productive at work and/or involved in community activities and organizations.	Care	40–65 years
8	**Ego integrity vs. despair** The ability to engage in contemplation and look back on life with a sense of closure and completeness.	Wisdom	65+

TRAUMA

It goes without saying that traumatic experiences can gravely impact children with anxiety. The loss of a loved one, a serious accident or another distressing event can set their progress back. Trauma shakes children's sensibilities, kicking the brain's emergency systems into high gear and making it difficult for the logical prefrontal cortex to remain focused and clear-minded. It's little wonder that, during times of crisis, reflection and good problem-solving elude our children.

The aftermath of a traumatic experience is a time when they need our support and their tools more than ever. Some children become more dependent. Their fears can escalate beyond what we thought possible, and they want to be with us and may ask to sleep in our bed. Other children recoil, becoming hard to reach and distracted. Both are signs that kids need our attentive care to help them feel secure and integrate what has happened.

This is a good time to soothe their body with physical comfort and closeness, as the opportunity to be vulnerable in our care prevents the emotional toughening so typical after trauma. Instead of becoming emotionally detached and frozen and shutting off their feelings, kids are able feel their distress and move through it, learning resiliency that bolsters the spirit, provides a sense of capability and allows them to gain confidence as they do.

Many parents find that retelling the story of the traumatic event in a healing light can help children to integrate, understand and accept the experience more readily. We've all experienced the healing power of storytelling from time to time: sometimes, a story erupts spontaneously around the dinner table about a funny or touching incident; at other times, the anecdote is delivered purposefully, such as at a memorial or a wedding. Storytelling helps us to understand our experiences and feel connected rather than isolated by them. Most importantly, this reframing process, which I like to call "say it to soothe it," allows children to make sense of and manage their emotions by helping to bring their left- and right-brain together. Encouraging children to *say* or name their emotions (right-brain) while recalling the facts of the event (left-brain) helps the two hemispheres to integrate what's happened and *soothe* the felt response. And reframing the experience by acknowledging what was learned further shapes a new meaning of the event and strengthens the sense that "we are capable of getting through difficult times."

CHANGES IN ROUTINE

Disruptions to the daily routine can cause distress for kids, and especially for children with anxiety. Even positive changes in the routine, such as hosting an out-of-town guest, going on vacation or celebrating a birthday, can bring significant upset. Think of times when you've wanted to create change in your own life, perhaps by committing to a regular exercise routine, adopting a more nutrition-conscious eating plan or making a vow to meditate more, but an unforeseen change derailed your plans. If, as you were beginning your new regime, you then went on a business trip, came down with the flu or hosted the in-laws for an impromptu visit (that lasted for weeks), your grand plans probably went by the wayside.

Similarly, we may find that just as our kids are finding relief from anxiety by using thought busters, visualization or belly breathing, a disruption comes along to throw them right off track. It's frustrating. But the beauty of this approach is that it allows us to explore mindfulness and connection even in those off-track moments. Noticing thinking traps and becoming aware of the negative internal dialogue that shows up during times of change can help children frame change in a more optimistic way.

Wherever possible, let children know about upcoming changes in routine ahead of time. Because we manage our children's lives so actively, we often expect them to just "go with the flow." We can easily lose sight of how important predictability can be, especially for children, who truly have very little control over what happens in their lives. As adults, our prefrontal cortex is fully formed and we can adapt, problem-solve and process next steps in a way that just isn't possible for our children—a fact we often forget. Providing children with support and information when a change, loss or challenge is on the horizon can help them to prepare internally for what's to come. The ideal time to start preparing children for a change will vary: some children need lots of time to ready themselves, while others will only worry unnecessarily with too much notice.

So often we direct our children's behavior on the fly: "You have to put your shoes on now," "It's time to eat your breakfast" and "We're going in five minutes." While we can't knock ourselves out with pre-emptive information, this kind of reactive prompting leaves little room for us to ask the kind of questions that will help our children mindfully tune in to what comes next and prepare themselves mentally and emotionally.

Sitting down with the family every week to talk about upcoming events is a great way to give our children a clear picture of who they will be with and when and can set the stage for a smooth week. Visual reminders are also especially good for young children. For example, try creating a picture schedule for a particular part of the day, such as bedtime. Playing together and taking pictures of each step in the bedtime routine can help us give our children a warm and positive connection with this difficult time of the day. Displaying those pictures on a poster board provides visual clues that can help their brain anticipate what's coming next. If they're having a difficult time staying on track, we can remind them, "Bedtime can be hard. Remember when we made those pictures of all the steps? Let's go and have a look at the ones we've done already and see what comes next."

The finest schoolteachers I've had the pleasure of knowing understand how important this advance preparation, or front-loading, is to the children in their classes. The walls of their classrooms are covered with images, schedules and visual reminders of special events, the classroom routine and expectations for behavior. The children's backpacks are regularly filled with notices outlining the week's events and inviting parents to chat about an upcoming science project or an outing to the local art gallery. These teachers share with me how frustrated they feel when they've been left out of the loop about a major life change that's upset the routine in a student's life, wishing they had been better equipped to understand why the child seemed less focused, more teary or withdrawn. Teachers too need front-loading to help their students integrate changes or challenges. After all, they provide an extension of our parental care.

Embracing challenges as opportunities for change

I love the quote: "If it doesn't challenge you, it won't change you." I have no idea who first coined the phrase, but I'm grateful for these powerful and motivating words. It's true that when we (and our children) face and overcome new challenges, we grow new neural circuitry that helps us to become more adaptable and resilient and that will bring greater vitality to our lives. Without challenge, and the anxiety that can accompany it, we simply wouldn't evolve as individuals.

Many of us struggle to know when to hold our ground and encourage our children to push through anxiety, and when it's time to back off. Making that call isn't an exact science, and it requires a certain level of faith in our parenting that can be shattered when our children aren't fully thriving. Encouraging our children to lean up against their fears runs counter to our urge to protect them. And our children are hardwired to tune in to our reactions to determine whether or not they're safe to face the thing

Fact: The average time a person waits to seek help for an anxiety disorder is more than ten years.

that challenges them. By reining in our own self-doubt and trusting our parenting judgment, we can give them the solid guidance they seek. Reminding ourselves and our children that the challenge will change them in wonderful ways can fill us with the confidence we need to move forward.

Dealing constructively with co-parenting woes

We'd like to think that all parents are co-operative, understanding and warm towards each other, and that we are continually working in partnership to prevent or relieve anxiety and stress in our children. But that ideal isn't always the case. Co-parenting is difficult at the best of times and can be made much more so if one parent is absent, erratic, unreliable, hostile or doesn't share the values or commitment of the other. Further challenges can arise if one or both of us is without a partner, newly single, re-partnering or blending with another family.

Although research on anxiety has largely ignored the role the family system plays in the development of children, some studies such as those of Akiho Tanaka and colleagues in the *Journal of Interpersonal Violence* have supported what many of us commonly believe by showing that children in high-conflict households have higher rates of anxiety. Kids who are highly anxious can be very sensitive to their environment, acutely picking up on parents' frustration and anger. It's not unusual for them to blame themselves for adult conflict and tension and to internalize their guilt as "all their fault."

Children of divorced or separated parents share similar difficulties; with those life changes may come the constant change of homes, variable approaches to child rearing and an extra financial pressure, and these can take a psychological toll on kids. Similarly, when one caregiver displays a lack of conscientiousness or attention to children's needs, the other parent may feel implicitly that any good intentions to support the kids' growth are being sabotaged. Allowing children to stay up late, packing their diet with sugars and simple carbohydrates, forgetting to have them complete their homework (yet again), allowing a full weekend of violent video games and playing fast and loose with their schedules can not only raise anger in the co-parent but lead to a fear that it will undermine the progress children have made up to that point.

As parents and significant others in our kids' lives, we can compensate greatly by displaying our own self-awareness, attention to connection and good coping skills. It can be tough to find ourselves in one of these situations, but by taking a breath and doing our very best to keep our cool, we can convey to our children that every human being and every family has vulnerability at its core and that while relations don't always go smoothly, we all have the option to step back from anger and reactivity. Then we can focus instead on defusing the competition with our co-parent by demonstrating to our children that being close with one of us does not need to interfere with a closeness with the other. In other words, we can reassure our children that they don't have to choose between loved ones and then feel guilty because of it: each parent, step-parent or grandparent can provide unlimited closeness and influence without distancing the other.

When we are consistently attentive, authentic and mindful of our values and behavior, our children will internalize that there is a better way to react when we are angry or hurt. As they grow, kids do apply what they've learned in our care: they will remember to do their homework on their own, go to bed without being prompted, ask for fruits and veggies over a hot dog and make wise moral choices when faced with difficult decisions.

Attending to our own emotional needs

At times, we can feel so burdened by the everyday demands for attention, soothing and crisis intervention that we wonder, "How long will this go on?" When we're deep in the parenting trenches, it's easy to lose sight of the fact that our children will be on to the next stage sooner than we can imagine. The fourth-graders will become busy teenagers soon enough and everything we've learned together will take them into adulthood.

Holding compassion for ourselves is one of the most powerful ways to bolster our own resilience when we are at our wits' end. Compassion for self moves us past shame and into a far more strengthening stance. It honors and acknowledges how much we're doing already: rewiring our parenting relationship and implementing new strategies, winning our children's trust and cooperation, and helping our children transform their negative anxiety into resiliency. It's a major undertaking and an empowering commitment that's well worth recognizing, regardless of the degree of success we are seeing at any one point. The truth is that we don't always hit the mark as parents. We have "off" days and times when we're so emotionally lit up that we lose it altogether. During our most challenging times, it's important to acknowledge what an immense responsibility parenting is and call in our support systems.

When it comes to seeking help, many of us struggle with guilt-driven internal messages such as, "I should be able to handle this on my own," "My child only wants me" or "There really is no one who can help." Truthfully, we were never meant to parent on our own, cut off from the support of multiple generations. Humans are designed to help each other and band together to raise future generations, and by asking for a hand, we're connecting with the "it takes a village" mindset our ancestors helped build into our genetic code. We are socialized to care for our young, but according to research across a variety of scientific disciplines, including studies by David Geary and Mark Flinn published in *Parenting: Science and Practice,* forging strong helping relationships has been the key selective pressure needed to ensure that our offspring survive. Our children in turn pass this magnificent genetic quality on to the next generation.

I'm fascinated by studies of fieldwork being done in Papua New Guinea, Tanzania and the Kalahari Desert, where ethnographers are living among tribes and remote clans. Allo-parenting (shared caregiving) is the norm in these societies. From their first hour, babies are cared for by as many as eight eager tribe members. Fieldwork carried out by Jared Diamond, an American scientist and award-winning geographer, shows that attachment-focused parenting reinforces what our ancestors already knew to be sound: holding our children, soothing their cries, practicing communal parenting and allowing for learning through natural consequences rather than forceful punishment all play a role in raising children who are more confident, competent and eventually autonomous. Sadly, we've all but lost this sense of shared responsibility in the Western world. Fragmented extended families and the demands of daily modern life may not allow us to practice the kind of baby-on-the-belly parenting seen in the Papuans, but there is much we *can* do to bring more allo-parenting into our fold.

Building a team of supports will not only help keep us from reaching (or exceeding) our wits' end, it will also help our children develop a confidence and sense of inner security that is simply not possible when they rely emotionally on one person alone. In the next chapter, we'll talk about a few ways to expand our children's tribe through school supports and parent allies.

NINE
....

AT HOME IN THE WORLD: SCHOOL AND SOCIAL SETTINGS

Social connectedness is one of our most powerful instruments for building resilience and emotional healing. Anxiety makes us less emotionally available to bond with others in all kinds of relationships. Children struggling with anxiety often feel different, lonely and easily criticized, so even just going "out to play" can be overwhelming. And as family members, we can feel held hostage socially, as we worry that our children may not be able to manage at a family gathering or a social event, and our evenings are often cut short when our children reach their tipping point. The resulting isolation is one of the heaviest burdens anxiety places upon children and the whole family.

Sharing information outside the family

I honestly believe that if we talked more about our vulnerabilities, we would all become stronger. Through our silence, we can lose sight of the fact that many others are facing the same struggles, and talking openly about the problem often leads us to discover that support may be closer at hand than we realize. But knowing how and when to reach out can be difficult because it involves a certain amount of risk. As parents, many of us are used to sharing openly with other parents, teachers and family members but we often forget that our children want emotional privacy. And not everyone is comfortable talking about anxiety, equipped to understand it and predisposed to help us deal with it. Figuring out when, why and with whom to share information about our children's anxiety takes some careful thought. The last thing we want to do is inadvertently violate our children's trust.

Fact: Children with mental health disorders are stigmatized more severely than adults by both adults and other children. In a large study of American parents, 30% said they would not want their child befriending a child with depression or attention deficit hyperactivity disorder (ADHD).

Including our children in the conversation about who to bring into the fold about their anxiety sends the message that we respect their need for privacy, and that they have some control over important decisions regarding their well-being. Our children may also need our help to better understand how others in their life fit into the picture, including the kinds of support they can provide. Just like when they were infants and another adult reached out to hold them, our kids are expectantly looking to us for cues to tell them whether or not they are safe. When our kids see our trust in others, they too will learn to trust.

One of the most helpful actions we can take to support our children is to select a "go-to" adult in every environment they spend time in. We can't always be there to buffer our children and support their steps towards resilience, but arranging for an understanding substitute to fill in for us during tough times can make all the difference for children whose anxiety is getting the best of them. Choosing "go-to" adults often happens intuitively, but it can be helpful to consider the following questions:

‣ *Who do we need to involve?* Adults who spend large amounts of time with our children should always be made aware of difficulties our kids are facing. Teachers and daycare workers will especially appreciate being kept in the loop. Whether or not we share with coaches, occasional babysitters, music teachers and people our children see less frequently will depend largely on whether the anxiety is actively interfering with their time together, and whether our children feel it would be helpful.

‣ *How much information is "too much information"?* Deciding what and how much to share with our children's team can be a tough call; there's a fine line between privacy and advocacy. Some parents guard their privacy fiercely, fearing their children may be treated differently. Others share more information than is necessary, running the risk of leaving their children feeling embarrassed or exposed. Asking ourselves *why* we're sharing the information and *what purpose* it serves in addressing the problem is a good way to gauge how much to share. Being clear about what we're asking for and not being afraid to follow up if we walk away without a solution or plan are also important steps.

Bringing the school on-side

I often hear stories from parents about school meetings that leave them feeling that they're living in a completely different reality from everyone else. They share their worries about their children's anxiety only to hear: "Your child is doing perfectly fine in the classroom." These parents feel it's "crazy-making" to explain how their children arrive home teary, needy, irritable or complaining of stomachaches and then have some teachers turn around and tell them it's a home-based problem; after all, the difficulty only shows up there. The opposite can also be true. Children who seem to be managing just fine at home may become highly distressed at school, disrupting the entire classroom and leaving teachers struggling to help them cope.

Advocating for children can mean many things: helping our children's teachers understand who our children *are* and what they may be facing, asking for resources, building a team around our kids and working through unhelpful attitudes about how our children are managing at school. The primary goal for parents and teachers alike is to help kids navigate their way through their educational experience in a positive way, but our skill, knowledge, emotional acuity and personal vantage points can vary immensely. Children spend more than 1,000 hours per year at school, so while it may take some work to create the kind of honoring connection we're looking for, building a relationship with our children's teachers based on mutual support and solidarity is well worth the time and effort.

Over the past twenty years of advocating for children within the school system, including my own children, I've learned that the relationship parents have with their children's teachers can go a long way. When teachers know that parents are *involved,* willing to work with them as a team and appreciate their efforts, most become mightily invested in helping children overcome their struggles. Of course, some teachers will go the extra mile regardless, but when we keep the lines of communication open, set specific goals and meet regularly to discuss progress, we put in place the checks and balances that keep everyone wholeheartedly committed.

Staying focused on our mutual intention to support our children allows us to reach out and communicate with integrity. While we may have moments of frustration, particularly if we feel our children's teacher is judging or mishandling difficult situations or isn't following through on an agreement, it's best to avoid a forceful approach, which will only put everyone on the defensive. Keep in mind, teachers often have insights and suggestions we haven't yet thought of, and these suggestions are well worth considering given the amount of time teachers spend with our children.

Tips for parent/teacher meetings

▸ *Set up a regular meeting time.* While teachers are often will-ing to meet on an as-needed basis, regular meeting times help ensure children are making consistent academic and emotional progress. If meeting during school hours is not possible, a chat over Skype or Facetime during the lunch hour might be an alternative.

▸ *Ask questions.* Knowing how children are doing generally and whether any indications of their anxiety are showing up in the classroom can help everyone to better under-stand the full range of our kids' triggers and anxious behaviors. Find out what the teacher is doing in the classroom to help the whole class manage anxiety. Some teachers incorporate regular mindfulness practice using programs like MindUP by the Hawn Foundation to set the stage for greater awareness, inner calm, empathy and understanding.

▸ *Share information.* Discussing our children's anxiety symptom checklist (page 71) with their teachers helps them to understand the many ways anxiety shows up in our children.

▸ *Put it in writing.* Letting teachers know about the tools and skills we're working on with our children at home can help them to reinforce these strategies in the class-room. Providing this information in writing helps to track goals and gives a concrete reference point they can go back to again and again.

▸ *Discuss alternatives.* Ask how the teacher manages circle time or group games. Children who are afraid of speak-ing out or getting the answer wrong will only shut down if pressured, but allowing closed-ended questions (with yes/no answers) or using a signal to let children know that their turn is coming up can encourage participation. Similarly, ask whether there are opportunities for kids to share knowledge on topics about which they are most confident. If children are afraid of public speaking, making a video can be a great alternative.

▸ *Talk about classroom protocols.* Here are some tips to suggest:

  ▸ Seating children with anxiety next to a friend can help make them feel more secure. And, when planning changes to the classroom arrangement, allowing them to have some choice about where or with whom they're situated can give them a sense of security.

  ▸ Children with test anxiety can become so distressed they freeze up. Giving them more time on tests can ease the pressure; in fact, just knowing the extra time is there if they need it can often be enough to help them relax. You may also want to suggest they take tests in another room so they don't get nervous looking at other children.

▸ Unstructured times are often the most difficult for children with social anxiety. During lunch and recess, make sure kids have an assigned buddy to call on—an older student can act as a peer mentor when younger children are feeling lonely or isolated.

▸ I'm a big fan of parent volunteers. Our presence in the classroom, library or playground may be deeply reassuring for our children. While we can't always be there, making a point of volunteering whenever we can is well worth our time and effort.

Having our children's teachers as part of the support network can help us access other resources within the school to reduce our children's symptoms of anxiety when they are in the classroom. Most schools are well versed in child anxiety and will have strategized for other kids. They may have a quiet room and/or resource workers for children who need a break from the class, or they may provide noise-cancelling headphones that can help kids to focus more intently on the tasks at hand. These resources and tools can help children to blossom and thrive both in their academic endeavors and in their extra-curricular activities.

Having children assessed by an educational child psychologist every few years can help identify areas of strength and weakness and strategies for managing gaps in learning. Carefully integrating any specific learning recommendations into individual education plans can go far in ensuring our children are well supported, especially if they also have a learning disability. Team meetings with the principal, primary teacher, psychologist, learning assistance teacher, and any other support staff whose roles and responsibilities are well articulated will help ensure our children's mental health and academic needs remain in focus. Bringing in these professional allies can be an amazingly effective way to better arm educators with the information they need to understand our children's needs. Whenever I've advocated for my own children at school, I've assumed that being a mental health professional should lend extra credibility to my perspective. However, in every teacher's eyes (and rightly so), I'm just another mom advocating for the needs of her kids. When I bring in an impartial third-party professional, this objective opinion carries more weight. Similarly, when I advocate on behalf of my clients, I see a greater responsiveness in teachers.

Studies by Dieter Wolke, Sarah Woods and others published in the *British Journal of Developmental Psychology* and by Jean A. Baker in the *Journal of School Psychology* have indicated time and time again that children who have positive experiences at school and who are actively engaged both there and in their community show lower levels of anxiety and stress and demonstrate healthier coping strategies. Supporting children at school with a "go-to" person they can trust can make the difference between a great year socially, emotionally and academically and a terrible one. If the children's classroom teacher isn't the best fit, another staff member can fill that role. When children know they can reach out to an adult who consistently looks out for their emotional needs, it's much easier for them to settle into learning. And if that chosen "allo-parent" is willing to adopt some of the mood-, thought- and body-regulation tools being practiced at home, that's even better.

Using parent-supported peer connection

Normal rites of childhood such as play dates and sleepovers can become far more complex for children with anxiety because these activities require two of the very skill sets—anxiety management and social skills—that these kids find challenging. However, because children with anxiety often avoid after-school activities such as team sports or clubs, arranging activities that allow our kids to connect with others becomes even more important. The key to success is parent-supported peer connection.

The usual drop-off-and-disconnect play date involves us dropping our kids off at another child's home or a daycare or other supervised facility and leaving them to play on their own with other children. We may be in the same building—or we may leave—but we are not actually involved. In a parent-supported play date, we support our children's peer attachment with a watchful eye, implicitly sending the message, "I'm here to lend support and set limits while you practice healthy separation." At times, that may mean stepping back to let children figure some things out on their own. At other times, coaching our children through a challenging moment or intervening when we notice them becoming overwhelmed is what intuitively feels right. Creating well-supported social time allows us to keep an eye on the interaction between our children and their peers and step in when any of the children's boundaries are being ignored for too long.

While it may be tempting to do the "drop and go" when it comes to play dates or sleepovers, taking the time to make connections with other parents beforehand is important. Most host parents want to understand the children they're caring for. And while it's good for kids to be exposed to different approaches in other families, finding safe and trusted parenting allies who understand the needs of our children is particularly important for kids struggling with anxiety. It can be helpful to talk privately with other parents ahead of time to cue them to common triggers or fears and to let them know what quells those anxieties. If children have difficulty managing their anxiety at another child's house, supporting the friendship by encouraging play dates in their own home is a great solution until they better develop their coping skills or until the friendship is well established.

When children are anxious, they can be prone to both being bossed around and being bossy—the former arising from a loss of protective instinct and the latter from a disconnection from their feelings for others. Parents describe to me how hard it is to see their children led about in the playground, at times playing the most humiliating of roles. For children held hostage by their own anxiety, the terror of speaking out can easily override their need to stand up and say, "No, I won't be the dog again and I don't want you to pull me by a pretend leash" or "Stop running away when I try to play with you. I feel really upset when you do that." It's easy to interpret bossiness, bullying and cruelty to others as children's urge to control. Recently, experts have come to view the problem more deeply; we now know that when children become desensitized to others' cues, it is often because they feel disconnected themselves. Their controlling behavior is a veiled and misguided attempt to feel they matter to others, and their aggression is often an attempt to get close to a certain child by alienating another. Whether our kids are being bossed or being bossy themselves, the vulnerability at the core points to a need for us to provide unconditional attachment, healthy limits and some social coaching when required.

HOW TO HELP OTHER KIDS UNDERSTAND

At times, we may need to act as our children's translator, letting other children know why ours are having a tough moment. Saying, "Kim would rather play inside because there are lots of bees out today and they make her uncomfortable" or "David feels more comfortable sleeping at home. Maybe you could come sleep at our house instead?" can create a bridge of understanding between children and may even open up a discussion about how each of them experiences fears. Better yet, we can help our children to practice explaining their fears themselves in a way that feels comfortable for them. The more they're able to practice talking about their powerful feelings, the more inoculated from those fears they will become.

Whether or not our children decide to tell a certain friend about their anxiety depends on many factors: their age, how well they know the other child, whether the child has shared their own personal information in the past, and whether they tend to gossip about other friends. Children with anxiety can be reticent to share their feelings because it leaves them feeling vulnerable and exposed, and they fear receiving insensitive reactions. Children who already *feel* different don't want to be *seen* as different, so gently encourage opening up to others, but let kids take the lead on when and to whom. Here are some words we can give our children to describe what they're going through:

▸ Sometimes I worry a lot—it's like my brain gets stuck on a worry channel and the remote won't let me change it.

▸ It's like my brain tells my body I'm in danger when I'm not—
my heart goes really fast and I feel really scared even when
there's nothing wrong.

▸ I get these ideas in my head that something bad is going to
happen and I can't convince my brain that everything is okay.
It makes it hard to go on sleepovers, but it's getting better.

▸ It's like a false alarm goes off in my brain and I have to try
and turn it off so I feel okay again.

Nurturing emotional intelligence

When I work with teens who suffer from anxiety, I'm often struck by
how aloof and distant they can seem and how much harder I have to
work to reach them emotionally. In time, I learn about how their fear
of being criticized or making a mistake has led them down a path of
hypercontrol, perfectionism and disassociation from others. I hear
their parents describe how insensitive they can be, how they seem
unable to fully grasp the impact of their comments on other people.

Many of these teens were children with heightened emotional
sensitivity. As they faced their anxiety, sometimes as a result of teasing or being unable to grasp social cues, they began to cope by
developing powerful brain responses to protect themselves against
vulnerability. In essence, they shut themselves off to the feelings
that provoked anxiety, and by blocking those feelings they became
unable to feel empathy or sense emotion in others. This emotional
toughness reduces children's awareness and vitality, shuts down
their capacity for joy, curiosity and connectedness, and prevents
them from taking the social risks so necessary to grow and learn.
Eventually this emotional hardening crystallizes into a rigid defense
mechanism and becomes part of their identity.

DESTRUCTIVE DEFENSE MECHANISMS

In our work together, I hold hope that my young clients are able to
soften their heart and let go of their destructive defenses in order to

access and release the pain underneath. I know they're returning to themselves when I see their eyes well up; many haven't cried for as long as they can recall. Parents, too, can help prevent children from becoming emotionally tough. Through us, teenagers who have already reached that point can still find a safe space in which to deal with their underlying pain. Children learn emotional resilience through their parents. Softening our own emotional hardening, having the courage to be vulnerable and learning together through adversity helps kids overcome their self-protective mechanisms and develop stronger emotional intelligence.

RULES OF ENGAGEMENT

Countless studies, including a 1995 study by Daniel Goleman, the leading expert in the study of emotional intelligence, or EQ, have shown that emotional and social skills far outweigh academic intelligence in their long-term advantage in academic success and overall happiness. In fact, Goleman shows that developing emotional intelligence improves self-awareness, confidence, empathy and positive behavioral choices. Social situations are a complex choreography of unspoken interpersonal rules that can be difficult enough for adults to navigate, let alone children. Bolstering our children's awareness of these rules gives them some protection from even the most volatile peer relationships.

Children have not yet developed the capacity to consciously maintain long-term friendships, and so they may be best friends one day but not the next. And the criteria for whether kids are "in" or "out" can be mercurial and impulsive, making friendship a necessary but risky prospect for any child. For children whose tolerance to stress is already low, this vulnerability to peer rejection can feel even stronger. And as our kids wrestle with these fears of rejection and the unbearable feeling of isolation that might result, they can easily feel compelled to quash any unique and naturally spontaneous expressions.

We also know that children facing heightened anxiety are less skilled in a wide array of social tasks. While the underlying reason isn't yet clear, it's most likely that either they haven't had enough practice using their skills or that their anxiety is inhibiting their brain's ability to fully access higher-order thinking. While we naturally develop many of the tools that connect us to others through our parent-child attachment or through learning by example, some interpersonal skills such as the ability to understand different perspectives, empathize with others and solve problems, can and should be taught. Just as we prompt our toddlers to answer when someone asks their age or to shake someone's hand when it's offered or to say "excuse me" after belching, our children and teenagers need coaching too.

As the mother of a fifteen-year-old, I can say honestly that social-emotional coaching is an ongoing task. When parents act as emotional translator, speaking the language of emotion and body awareness, we are teaching our children the most essential tool to regulate emotion, thoughts and behavior: the ability to name their experience. Our children need us to witness, describe and then process the experience with them. And when they come to us, knowing we'll help them navigate a problem that's arisen with a friend, teacher or coach, we know we've hit the sweet spot in our parenting relationship.

TEASING AND BULLYING

When I think about my eldest son as a preschooler, I keenly remember his gentle way, easy smile and sensitive temperament. He was shocked each and every time other preschoolers would push, grab or even bite out of frustration. It never made sense to him that a *friend* could be so hurtful; it simply wasn't part of his nature. No matter how much I encouraged him to "use his words" to assert himself, his only response to this situation was to *freeze*. He was under threat and his survival systems were running strong.

As he grew older and moved through the primary school years, it wasn't uncommon for him to arrive home with long stories about kids teasing each other mercilessly in the playground. This was a "survival of the fittest" mentality he couldn't understand. When others hurt, he hurt, and while he wasn't a victim of bullying himself, witnessing it was perhaps equally damaging. In time he learned to take a stand for the underdog, as all children must if bullying is to stop, but it wasn't until his first year of high school that he fully gained the self-confidence to override the anxiety that had kept him silent when he'd most needed to speak out.

Whereas bullying was once thought a rite of passage, it's now recognized through data collected by The National Center for Educational Statistics and Bureau of Justice that one out of four kids is deeply affected. Studies by Young-Shin Kim and colleagues published in the *Archives of General Psychiatry* tell us that these children are suffering academically and mentally, with increased risk of anxiety, depression, sleep problems, and thoughts of self-harm and suicide. When kids internalize these personal attacks, it creates a complicated cascade of emotional, physical and bio-chemical responses that can impair the body's immune system and the brain functions that govern the body.

Teaching our kids the assertiveness skills needed to say "no" can preserve them from experiencing this violation of self and it can also protect their safety. Another way to prevent them from being victimized or from wanting to dominate is cultivating an attachment known in psychology as "closeness through signifi-cance." This feeling that we matter is at the center of the parent-child relationship and it is an important model for our interaction with others. Our kids' reliance on us and desire to be held in our care help ensure the balance in the parenting hierarchy. In all our relationships, emotional boundaries tell us where one person ends and the other begins, which helps to maintain the natural order and keep our dignity intact. With strong boundaries in place, parents are parents and children are children who accept our guidance without being threatened by it. These same boundaries also help ensure that the power balance among children remains a healthy dance of give and take in which no one child has the upper hand for long, and in which caring trumps domination.

Children facing anxiety often have compromised emotional boundaries, which sets them up for vulnerable interactions with the world around them. As their bodies are on high alert dealing with perceived threats to their survival, children with anxiety find that decision-making and thinking on their feet become more difficult. Imagine you're seven years old and wrestling with immobilizing levels of anxiety. Now consider what it might be like to be away from your parents and facing another child who has chosen to make embarrassing remarks about you at every chance. Then imagine that child excluded you from group activities, asked your friends not to talk to you and made mean-spirited comments about you on the Internet. Now, imagine that you remained silent about it all. This complete domination of one person by another mentally and emotionally for a prolonged period of time is the kind of boundary violation that can haunt children, especially those who are already anxious and emotionally vulnerable.

Imagine yourself as that same child, still fending off anxiety's sting, but this time you're able to take a deep breath and confidently tell a peer who's making nasty remarks, "Your opinions aren't important to me at all" or "I didn't hear that. Can you say that a bit louder, in front of the teacher this time?" Imagine yourself going directly to the supervision aid or the teacher if the insults continue. Picture coming home and telling your parents the story of what happened, feeling their compassion as they listen keenly to you. And then your parents do something that will empower you for life—they help ensure your boundaries are respected and they take steps to deal with the problem, head on.

When it comes to teaching our children assertiveness skills, we can only share what we know ourselves. When we notice where our own boundaries might be being blurred and mindfully expand into that space, holding true to ourselves, not only do we hold firm to our own "bottom line" in conflict situations, we become "centered as self." It's a state of being that tells others non-verbally that we know who we are and we are not open to being manipulated.

A child who cannot say "no" to us cannot say "no" to others. In his book *Hold On to Your Kids: Why Parents Need to Matter More than Peers,* attachment specialist Gordon Neufeld describes "counterwill" as "a natural response to a child's need for autonomy and an instinctive resistance to being forced." It shows up passively when our children dig their heels in and actively when they're openly defiant. It's understandable that our children are oppositional at times; they're testing limits and asserting their self. But when counterwill doesn't easily subside, it may mean our children's desire to please has been overridden by the "power over," or forceful parenting response, that so often leads to power struggles. When kids are no longer looking to please, it often means they've lost a feeling of connection, and validating their emotional experience can go a long way towards creating openings of understanding. By looking past the defiance and using our ability to soothe and support, we allow our children to practice their "no" and at the same time hold our parenting ground. Allowing children to have boundaries with us doesn't mean giving in; on the contrary, it means meeting kids where they're at emotionally and giving them a voice while upholding expectations for conduct. Counterwill is a key emotional response and behavior to protect our children against harmful outside forces such as negative peer influence and fades as children develop. If their attachment is healthy, our children replace counterwill with interpersonal confidence and assertion.

While we all have a responsibility to support children who are being victimized, we are sometimes too quick to label the problem

CLEAR FLUID BOUNDARIES

Good for all ages

Materials needed: none

In chapter 4, we learned all about the reasons that cause us to take on the emotional states of the people around us. This "emotional contagion" is great when the people around us are in a good mood, but it's not such a good thing when someone around us is in a lousy mood. Creating a "clear fluid boundary" that defines where we stop and other people begin can be a great tool to help children. When we explain that everything inside the boundary is theirs and that everything outside belongs to everyone else, they know that the thoughts, feelings and judgments of others don't have to come in. Kids love their clear fluid boundary, and it's one of the tools they tend to remember most (little kids call it their bubble). They especially like to use it when we get mad because it gives them a way to remain emotionally separate and safe when our own stress chemicals surge.

STEP 1: Remind children that when someone else's words or actions enter our personal space, it can really affect the way we think and feel. So to make sure we're not matching the hurtful or negative comments, we can create a "clear fluid boundary" that separates our feelings, thoughts and experiences from those around us.

as "bullying." In truth, there is a big difference between a hurtful incident and ongoing bullying behavior. With all the recent talk about identifying bully behavior in the school system and in our communities, children sometimes lose sight of this crucial differ-

STEP 2: Ask children to put out their arms and notice their clear fluid boundary; it's like a bubble all around them. Now have them put down their arms and notice that it's still there, but this time notice that it has a color to help them see where it is.

STEP 3: Now play it out! Warn kids that you're going to pretend to be angry or say something grumpy or negative, like "What a lousy coach" or "This is the worst day *ever.*" Invite them to put up their clear fluid boundary and *bounce* that negative emotion away so it doesn't enter their bubble. Invite children to pretend to be angry with you, so you can practice having your boundary in place too.

STEP 4: Next, look at what happens when the boundaries are not in place. Announce that you're going to pretend to be mad again and invite kids to notice what it's like when they forget to put up their clear fluid boundary. Don't be surprised if you find children reminding you, "Mommy, are you sure your bubble is up?" Not only does it feel better for kids to know how to separate themselves from our strong emotions, it's reassuring to know they can have their own big feelings without burdening us. The idea here is we can feel understood and care for others without *matching* them. In fact, matching only interferes with our ability to see clearly what our children are going through.

ence. I've seen many young clients crushed by being accused of being a dreaded "bully" by one of their peers, only to discover after peeling away the details that clearly their hurtful behavior was the result of a temporary misjudgment. When our children are mistreated by others, it's helpful to remind them that while their hurt feelings are certainly valid, labeling another child as a bully can stick for a very long time. Instead of validating children's knee-jerk reactions prematurely, give them a hand in distinguishing the difference.

WHAT DOES BULLY BEHAVIOR LOOK LIKE?

‣ Bullying is a *pattern* of behavior intended to make another person feel scared, uncomfortable or hurt. It's both a systematic and deliberate attempt to diminish or intimidate the victim.

‣ Bullying can be physical, verbal, social or cyber.

‣ Bullying may look like name calling, online impersonation, spreading rumors or gossip, threatening, using racial slurs, physically hurting another person, stealing belongings, excluding individuals from groups, sending harmful texts, posting harmful videos and touching without consent, among others.

Fact: Over a quarter (28%) of students in Ontario report having been bullied at school at least once during the school year. In nearly all cases, the bullying has been verbal rather than physical.

Offer children on the receiving end of bully behavior some tools to protect themselves from vulnerability. Walking confidently, looking the other child in the eye, speaking up for themselves and staying close to sympathetic others are all ways for our children to say, "You can't rattle me." By remaining emotionally tuned in as we help our children build the tools they need, we're helping them to avoid becoming the victim of another child's maladaptive coping strategies. Better yet, our children will be turning towards us rather than their peers for safety, support and guidance. So we can take the lead, trust our parenting instincts and talk often about all the savvy ways our children listen to themselves and remain outside of playground hierarchies of dominance.

When bully behavior shows up in our own children, it can be terribly upsetting. We can be tempted to "read them the riot act." Children acting out in this way need care and attention, not punishment. They need help to understand why they're striving so hard for dominance and why they're feeling so vulnerable that they've shut down their awareness of the full impact of their actions. When children harden their feelings of compassion, it indicates a deep wound; they aren't emotionally shutting down on purpose. They're usually lashing out at one person to get closer to another. Instead of cracking down on them with the force of anger, we can re-affirm our attachment with them by reintegrating them into the parent-child hierarchy. Simply put, our children need to know we're in charge, firm and unwavering in our supervision both at home and at school (which may mean checking in with the teacher regularly). Our next task is to soften their emotional hardening by creating a space for re-connection; from there, tenderness and vulnerability can re-emerge. From the heart of our connection will come the kind of moral awareness, responsibility and empathy for others from which they have shut themselves off.

TEN

LIFESTYLE AS A ROUTE TO MIND-BODY HEALTH

Renowned speaker, author and addictions specialist Dr. Gabor Maté writes that: "Mind and body are not separable . . . and our immune system does not exist in isolation from daily experience." Our lifestyle choices are integral to our well-being, yet many of us hold on tight to our habits, even when they're not in our best interest. Diet, sleep and exercise all contribute to our mental health, so a few simple changes can help keep us and our children's mind-body system in working order and stave off anxiety.

The food-mood connection

Feeding kids a nutritious diet is downright difficult for most parents, myself included. Children might choose to eat heartily one day and not the next. They might insist that asparagus is "gross" when they haven't even tried it, or that they can't eat their carrots because they've touched the mashed potatoes.

While we all understand the old adage "You are what you eat," we tend to lose sight of the fact that we also *feel* what we eat. What our children eat affects their thinking patterns, ability to sleep and especially their emotional well-being. Finetuning the family's eating habits can have a profound impact on anxiety levels and overall health at every age. Some key changes to what and when our kids eat can help to trigger powerful chemical and physiological changes in their brain, altering their behavior and emotions for the better.

EAT REGULARLY

Food is fuel. If our children skip meals altogether, we know we will find ourselves with tired and cranky youngsters on our hands. For kids, however, mealtime is often seen as boring—after all, they're being pulled away from the thing they love most, which is playing. It's not surprising they become master mealtime avoiders, and tableside power struggles can become a way of life. If it becomes a struggle to get children to the table for three square meals a day, a nutritious snack every four hours will help ensure their blood sugar level doesn't sink, and their mood right along with it.

START THE DAY WITH BREAKFAST

We've all heard the cliché that breakfast is the most important meal of the day, and science backs that up. Research has shown that eating breakfast helps kids perform better academically, get into less trouble at school and participate more often in class discussions. In 2008, the Feeding Our Future program tracked 6,000 Toronto-based students for two years and found those who were fed well-balanced meals had improved marks and better behavior.

Breakfast skippers have lower energy and a harder time paying attention, while breakfast eaters have fewer unhealthy cravings and are more likely to maintain a healthy weight. Complex carbohydrates and proteins can help combat our children's early morning craving for sugary cereal and improve their learning and overall success in the classroom, whereas a breakfast high in simple carbohydrates with little protein causes them to be sluggish.

Here are some time-savers for hectic early mornings:

1. **Make smoothies.** While they might look like milkshakes, smoothies are a brilliant way to blend in some extra nutrients—and kids love them. Prepare the ingredients the night before, then, in the morning, just blend and pour. Another great idea is to fill a muffin tray with an array of pre-cut fruits and vegetables, and invite kids to create their own recipe in the morning.

2. **Cook an extra-large batch of steel-cut oats.** Cooked oats are easy to reheat, so make a large pot early in the week and warm them up as required throughout the week. Add berries and plain low-fat yogurt to plain oats to ramp up the nutrients and add flavor.

3. **Thaw pre-made mixed-grain waffles or pancakes.** Make a big batch of these on the weekend, then freeze them to eat during the week. In the morning, pull them out of the freezer and pop them in the toaster. When warm, top them with peanut butter or raw nuts for extra protein and fruit compote for sweetness.

INCLUDE CARBOHYDRATES

Carbohydrates are the most misunderstood element in our diet, and the low-carb movement of the 1990s didn't help. Still, some carbs are better than others. Foods high in simple carbs such as white flour, soda, packaged cereal and candy add very little nutritional value to the body and should be avoided. In contrast, complex carbs, such as whole grains, vegetables and beans, are rich in fiber, vitamins and minerals, and act as the body's fuel for energy production. By choosing carefully, we can provide our children with the kind of carbohydrates, such as slow-burning oatmeal and whole grains, that produce serotonin, which improves mood, calms the mind and stabilizes appetite.

According to the American Academy of Pediatrics, carbs should make up 50 percent of our kids' overall daily food intake. A diet packed with complex carbs provides our kids with more energy, and helps them to feel happier and be more relaxed overall. If you are not already eating complex carbs, try substituting whole-grain pasta and breads, brown rice and air-popped popcorn for their old snacks, to help children adapt to the change. And avoid the simple carbs, including the refined and processed sugars that often hide in beverages such as sodas and sugar-added fruit juices. These lead to obesity and high blood pressure and crowd out foods rich in nutrients that support children's growth and brain development. According to the National Health and Nutrition Examination Survey conducted between 2001 and 2004, the average American consumes 22 teaspoons of refined sugar each day, or triple the recommended amount! Sugary drinks, as it turns out, create a resistance to leptin, the hormone that tells the body when we're full. Without the body signals necessary to let them know that enough is enough, children can easily drink spoonfuls of sugar, leaving them both hyper and hungry (yikes!). Instead, opt for water, nutritious green smoothies or low-fat cow's milk, which contains whey protein, an antidote to stress.

BALANCE THE NUTRIENTS

Nutrients are the vitamins, minerals, fats, carbs and proteins the body uses as fuel. A shortage of nutrients in the body can cause mood and anxiety troubles. For example, according to a recent report in the *Dartmouth Undergraduate Journal of Science,* getting too little thiamine (vitamin B1), which is found in cauliflower, eggs, cereal grains, beans, nuts and meat, is linked to a decrease in self-confidence and energy, poor mood and introversion, all of which can appear alongside anxiety. Low levels of iron, a mineral found in red meat, beans, eggs, oatmeal, soybeans and spinach, can cause fatigue, inattention, irritability and depression. Folic acid, a vitamin found in citrus fruits, nuts, beans, whole-wheat bread and dark leafy vegetables, helps maintain serotonin levels. A recent report by the *Journal of Adolescent Health* concluded that fewer than one in three kids is meeting daily requirements for fruit and veggie intake. To make sure kids are getting their daily dose, try keeping a variety of each in a bowl in a high-traffic area. I guarantee you'll find it empty at the end of the day.

Omega-3 fatty acids are key to a healthy diet. As well as staving off children's hunger, foods high in omega-3 fatty acids, such as fatty fish, walnuts, fortified eggs, peanut butter and homemade granola bars, help improve mood and memory. In fact, kids with low omega-3 levels are more prone to be pessimistic, act impulsively and feel down. One way to bring more omega-3s into the diet is to try an omega-3 scavenger hunt at the grocery store. Not long ago, I gave both of my boys a basket and a list of food items containing omega-3 fatty acids. It was fun to see them scouring the store and even more rewarding when they were willing to try the new healthy foods on their list—after all, they'd worked hard to find them.

The food-emotion connection

As parents, we naturally love to nurture our kids, especially with food. But eating can be a serious issue for kids with anxiety. Desperate to get them to eat, we might over-accommodate them and end up making two or even three dinners a night. It is much better for the whole family to eat the same meal, with the exception of super spicy foods. At least one item in any meal should be something the kids like, but our kids should *do their best* to try everything. Avoid power struggles, which send the message that we think we know our kids' bodies better than they do. Trust me when I say that children will not leave themselves malnourished if they're consistently given healthy food options.

INTRODUCE NEW FOODS SLOWLY

Keeping in mind that some children have heightened anxiety around trying certain foods, we can use exposure strategies to help introduce them to a wider variety of foods. I recently started seeing an eleven-year-old, and when asked what he'd like to gain from counseling, he told me: "I want to be able to eat more foods. I'm going away to summer camp and I'm worried I won't be able to eat the food there." Not only did the taste of many foods make him wriggle, he also couldn't handle certain textures. Mushy food was intolerable, and most fruits were out of the question. Together we made a list of his tolerable foods and ones he couldn't yet eat—a "no-go" food list that was remarkably long. We began by introducing new foods progressively, the way we might with a baby. He ate each new food every day in whatever portion he could manage until it became tolerable. Then we would introduce another new food and repeat the process. His determination was admirable, and he accomplished much of his goal by the time summer camp came around. He'd changed his mindset *and* made a commitment to his long-term health.

KEEP FOOD SEPARATE FROM OTHER ISSUES

As well as having a varied, nutritious diet, we also want our children to learn to listen to themselves, and that starts with listening to their body. When we say no to seconds or force our kids to finish a plate of food, we risk sending the message that they should ignore what their body is telling them.

Similarly, using food as a reward encourages children to see it as a way to deal with their emotions. Food can be a strong reinforcement, and most parents don't hesitate to use its powerful muscle. It's tempting to say, "If you finish your veggies, you can have your dessert." Children might interpret this as, "If you eat the yucky stuff, I'll give you the yummy stuff." Or worse yet, "If you're really brave and go to school, I'll put an extra cookie in your lunch." But making food into a prize for good behavior can lead to unhealthy lifestyle choices through the teenage years and into adulthood.

Instead, by offering at least one option we know kids will eat, exposing kids to new foods and having them try a taste of it and focusing on table time as a chance to connect with the family, we create a positive relationship with food for our children.

The food-social connection

Of all the support mechanisms we try to put into place for our kids, one of the most positive things we can do for them is also the simplest—eat meals together. Earlier in my life, I co-owned a few restaurants, which gave me a window into the lives of some brilliant chefs. Anytime I had a chance, I loved to interview them about their approach to feeding their families. While good nutrition wasn't always at the forefront of their minds, eating family meals together was. Research by Mary Spagnola and others shows that the benefits of family routines, like eating meals as a family, are staggering. Children gain self-esteem. They have larger vocabularies, healthier diets, better communication skills and higher grades. They are also less likely to be overweight and abuse drugs or alcohol.

Fact: Over one half of families with children in the United States eat together no more than three times a week, and some never do.

How do family meals make such a powerful difference in the overall health and well-being of children? Simply put, they make children feel more secure, connected and cared for. Sitting face to face, fork in hand with technological gadgets turned off, magic happens. Suddenly, the whole family is talking about that last ski vacation. Our older children might be asking us about when we met our partner, and our own questions are actually being answered. A family meal is a time when everyone is on the same playing field, and every opinion is heard. Dr. Dan Siegel describes it as a chance to shift from "me to we." Building children's family connections through these intentional moments wires their brain to expect warmth and connection—especially if we're setting that tone.

BRING CHILDREN INTO THE CULINARY FOLD

Whenever I run low on creative ideas for encouraging healthy eating, I consult my friend and nutrition guru, Alyssa Bauman. Alyssa lives and breathes healthy living and her kids are right on board. The trick is that she started good health practices from day one; from the moment her children could stand, they were stirring, washing, straining, cracking, pouring, measuring and juicing. Her family is proof that when children are included in preparation, they feel connected not only to us, but to their food. Children who participate in meal prep are more likely to enjoy eating what they've created. There's no better way to nurture our body, our family connection and our children's mental health.

Giving our kids a little culinary control can be another way to encourage a healthy attitude towards food. Give them room to explore and play in the kitchen, and we open up their curiosity and learning space—my youngest son's specialty is whole-grain sandwiches made with grilled organic chicken, raisins, tomatoes and whole-grain O's cereal for crunch (yum!). With experimentation comes confidence and pride in their ability to care for themselves and contribute to the family.

It's important to make sure the kitchen is full of healthy, nutritious food. Alyssa recently volunteered to come to my home and do a "kitchen cleanse," which involved assessing each item in my cupboard and refrigerator to purge problem food items from our lives. While I'll admit to being nervous about how many items would end up in the discard pile, the practice of mindfully assessing each and every item in our kitchen was more health-enhancing than intimidating. And including the children in the practice gave us all a sense of control over the process.

One of the main categories on the chopping block was packaged snacks, which are less nutritious and have tons of fat, sugar and sodium. Alyssa helped us create a list of healthy snack ideas to replace our usual grab-and-go ones. They're easy to make, so with a little luck and encouragement, kids will love to help prepare them. Here are a few of the highlights:

▸ Make a homemade antipasto platter. Cube cheese, roll up organic meats, put out some olives, assemble a dipping bowl of hummus and slice cucumbers into "chips." Let kids design the tray.

▸ Peel one banana per person and spread it with nut butter. Roll it in hemp seed hearts and cut it into wheels.

▸ Spread celery sticks with peanut butter or cream cheese. Top them with raisins to make "ants on a log."

▸ Stuff whole-grain pita pockets with cheese and Granny Smith apple slices. Add a dash of cinnamon.

▸ Mix together ready-to-eat cereal, dried fruits, goji berries and nuts in a sandwich bag for an on-the-go snack.

▸ Top unsweetened yogurt with crunchy homemade granola and sprinkle with blueberries.

▸ Make snack kabobs. Put cubes of cheese and grapes on pretzel sticks.

▸ Toast whole-grain waffles and top them with unsweetened yogurt and sliced peaches.

▸ Spread peanut or almond butter on apple slices.

▸ Sprinkle grated Monterey Jack cheese over corn tortillas. Fold them in half and microwave for twenty seconds. Top with salsa.

▸ Toss dried cranberries and chopped walnuts into instant oatmeal.

▸ Spread a favorite nut spread and honey on whole-grain wraps. Layer a fruit roll-up on top. Roll and cut into pieces.

▶ Make kale chips by drizzling fresh kale leaves with olive oil, setting them on parchment paper and baking at 300°F for eight to twelve minutes.

▶ Spread mustard on whole-wheat flour tortillas. Top with a slice of turkey, cheese and lettuce, then roll them up.

▶ Make mini pizzas. Toast whole-wheat English muffins or pitas, drizzle with pizza sauce and sprinkle with mozzarella cheese and diced vegetables.

The sleep solution

"Sophie's worst time of the day is always bedtime. Every night is a fight," a mother once told me. "We've tried reward programs, fixed up her room to make it a 'fairy palace' and finally took away her TV time with the hope she'd understand we were serious. My husband and I are exhausted by the end of the day. We have almost no time together, let alone time for ourselves. Most nights, I just give up and end up sleeping in her room."

This mother's story is a familiar one for many parents. Children have an inordinate amount of information running through their minds, crowding out the peace they need to let go and fall asleep. This is exponentially more difficult for children dealing with anxiety; however, working out a solution is key to kids' lifelong relationship with healthy sleep. We're only just starting to understand the link between children's sleep and mental health. When kids feel they haven't yet had enough time with parents, nighttime heightens the physical and emotional separation they've experienced throughout the day. However, when children feel our emotional accessibility, their nighttime panic lessens. They feel satisfied and less vulnerable. This is not to say a healthy level of attachment is the solution to all sleep problems. But it will help restore our children's sense of security and invite them to express their feelings of vulnerability.

The connection between sleep and overall brain health is undeniable. Sleep affects anxiety levels, as well as our ability to manage emotions, make connections, solve problems and focus. Without the requisite ten to eleven hours of sleep, schoolchildren aren't just facing a cranky day—if the problem continues long-term, their development is at risk. Their brains will lack the rest needed to grow optimally and integrate information. Their insulin levels and metabolism may become imbalanced, and their immune functions can become compromised.

While each child's experience of anxiety is different, those with clinical levels are highly prone to sleep disruption. Insomnia (difficulty falling asleep, staying asleep, or having restless and unsatisfying sleep) is one of the key symptoms of generalized anxiety disorder. And, while studies by Candice Alfano and colleagues show that 88 percent of children with generalized anxiety experienced some sort of sleep difficulties (55 percent experienced three or more types of disturbance), the exact nature or cause of the sleep problem is different for each one. For example, children with social anxiety might lie awake for hours thinking about an upcoming presentation or birthday party, or ruminating on what might happen at school the next day.

Anxiety disorders aside, most of us have had to spend a little extra time before bed soothing our children whose thoughts are stuck on the events of the day, mentally playing out upsetting situations. When our kids have a hard time falling asleep or staying asleep or when they wake too early, the play-based tools will help—CBT and mindfulness are the first lines of attack for sleep disruption. Add to that a practice of good sleep hygiene, and our children will learn to maintain a healthy sleep-and-wake cycle that maximizes their cognitive, emotional and physical abilities. We may even sleep better, too! The secret to changing nighttime habits involves creating a plan and sticking with it. Try including children in the solution and consider some of the following tips:

▸ **Practice good pre-sleep hygiene:** In this case I'm not referring to the bedtime brushing of teeth or washing up. Instead, cutting out computers, TV and other technological devices helps our kids calm their neurological system. We can use this time to read together, listen to relaxing music and wind down from the day (it's amazing how much connection comes with boycotting technology!). It almost goes without saying that we should also avoid any scary material, studying or activities that get our kids revved up.

▸ **Watch the mindset:** Children naturally open up emotionally right before bedtime; they're reviewing their day and have the quiet space to turn inwards. Engaging emotionally is a way to attach and be soothed by us at the most vulnerable time of the day. While it's rewarding to see our children share their thoughts and feelings rather than internalizing them, lengthy conversations about emotionally upsetting events can exacerbate sleep problems. The negative internal story often doesn't shut off once the conversation has ended. Validating their worry and reassuring them that we'll make time to talk about their concern in the morning may work for some. And writing the worry down shows our attention to their need in a concrete way. If persistent worries aren't subsiding, encourage "changing the channel" with a brief chat about the great things the next day will bring. I find that setting aside time for a worry earlier in the day helps prevent a prolonged emotional unloading at nighttime.

▸ **Break open the bubbles:** One of my favorite times of the day is right after dinner when everyone's tummies are settled and the whole family can relax. I steep a cup of tea, draw a bubble bath for my youngest and hang out on the floor as he decompresses and spontaneously begins to chat about his day. When he's in the bath, there's nothing to distract him and nowhere to go (plus I can fit in some yoga!). Knowing my days of bath-time chats are numbered, I savor every moment. Older kids who want privacy in the bath can enjoy setting the stage with bubbles, music and dimmed lights. Childhood memories of warmth, calming essential oils and time spent turning inwards will create a template for their automatic coping mechanism in the future.

▶ **Use the toolkit:** When children are stuck on irrational negative beliefs, unhelpful stories of the day or thinking traps, the play-based CBT tools in this book can help. One or two may be particularly effective, and we can choose to make those ones a natural and consistent part of our kids' sleep routine. Thought busters, visualization and progressive relaxation are potent ways to calm the brain system, which encourages better sleep. It can also be helpful to put self-supporting thoughts on cue cards, keep fear-fighting spray (page 115) close by and play relaxing music such as Quiet Spaces (relaxkids.com) or Dreamchild (joyfilledmusic.com).

▶ **Kick out the clock:** Clocks in bedrooms are a recipe for anxiety—they become a new source of stress as our children ruminate on how upset we will be because it's "so late."

▶ **Watch the lingerer:** Children are notorious nighttime lingerers with requests for a glass of water, a snack or another trip to the bathroom. Until I wised up to my own son's nighttime tricks, I was first in line to give in. After all, what parent feels good about children going to bed with hunger pangs or is able to turn down a request for "just one more hug?" It seemed that all the love, security and attention in our moment-to-moment connection just wasn't kicking the lingering habit. Instead, we instituted a nightly "last call for questions," which gave him the firm limits he needed to understand the evening could no longer be extend-a-play. If "last call for questions" isn't successful, firmly remind little lingerers: "I know you can stick with the plan. I'll give you lots of hugs in the morning." As part of that plan, decide together how many times to check in. Keep check-ins extremely low key; if youngsters are still awake, a soft "Love you, kiddo" or a little rub to their back is all that's needed.

▸ **Be clear about whose bedroom is whose:** I'm not a stickler about kids sleeping in their own bed. But for a sleep-deprived family, avoiding the musical beds game becomes important. Not only does it preserve our intimate life, but it also helps our children learn to enjoy their personal space. For kids with a fear of sleeping alone, we need to first dismantle the fear by building their tolerance to nighttime independence. By tucking them into their own bed, not ours, and extricating ourselves only as quickly as our children will tolerate, we build their confidence and ability to settle into sleep. Some parents start by sitting on the side of the bed for ten minutes using calming strategies (such as visualization or progressive relaxation) together, then graduate to having the kids practice on their own while the parents provide a supportive presence. By starting slowly, we can gradually distance ourselves by sitting on the floor, then at the door, then in the hallway and finally in the living room. Some parents use baby monitors to reassure their children they really can hear them if there's an emergency. And when our kids make their way into our bed in the middle of the night, it is important to try our best to return them to their bed. In time, their 2 A.M. visits should decrease in frequency. I promise you: once your children become teenagers, they really do outgrow their nighttime dependence.

▸ **Create a sleep-only zone:** Sleep clinics have a variety of proven methods to clean up sleep hygiene, and creating a sleep-only space is top of the list. When kids' bedrooms are filled with TVs, computers and lots of toys, the brain creates a powerful association between pleasurable, active play and the room itself. Few of us have the luxury of a playroom, but keeping toys and books neatly tucked away in opaque bins works just as well. Temporarily relocating play, homework and technological devices to another room can break the association and improve our children's sleep.

▶ **Frame bedtime as a gift:** Turning the conversation about bedtime into something positive can help change our children's internal story about it. Making bedtime a punishment will only exacerbate their negative narrative. Instead, we can model good bedtime behavior by talking about how much we're looking forward to hitting the pillow. Try asking children what they like about bedtime. Thinking about their fuzzy pajamas, their favorite stuffed animal or the fluorescent stars on their ceiling may be what they need to make them look forward to bedtime.

▶ **Introduce bedtime boredom:** A healthy dose of the mundane can be a potent antidote to our children's anxious nighttime mind. Along with the relaxation exercises in the play-based toolkit, we can teach them tricks like counting backwards, silently singing the same song over and over or breathing in a relaxing color and letting it fill their body. I once tried the cloud imagery (page 138) with my youngest son, and he promptly told me "That sounds like too much work. I'll just go to sleep."

▶ **Limit naps:** Long naps can disturb our children's internal sleep cycle, which can leave them feeling drowsy throughout the day and create difficulties falling asleep at night. Limiting nap time to twenty minutes can restore their energy during the day without robbing them of a good night's sleep.

▶ **Keep food in mind:** Eating right before bedtime can be a problem, especially for children who have difficulties falling and staying asleep. Try to avoid serving large meals just before bed, and avoid making drastic dietary changes while battling sleep-related issues. While they may be in our kids' best interest, changes to their food regime can temporarily exacerbate sleep problems. A better approach is to ease our children into dietary changes step by step, and monitor the effects on their sleeping habits. Caffeine can remain in the system for half the day, so avoid any sugar or caffeine, especially sodas, which often have high levels of both.

▸ **Get a move on:** There is a strong connection between sleep and activity. We'll discuss the benefits of an active life in greater depth later in this chapter, but it's worth mentioning now that physical activity is key to solving both our children's anxiety and their sleep habits. Vigorous activity, such as swimming or a good game of tag, is better undertaken early in the day. Relaxing and soothing exercise, such as yoga, before bed can be a great help in initiating a good sleep.

▸ **Lighten up:** Our bodies align with the natural cycle of the day, so exposure to natural sunlight maintains a healthy sleep cycle. Spending too much time indoors can send our children's internal clock into a tizzy, leading to sleepless nights and drowsy days. Vitamin D supplements have been shown to improve sleep problems and interrupted circadian rhythms, but consult with the children's doctor for recommended dosages.

MANAGING NIGHTTIME FEARS

Fear of the dark, strange noises, monsters under the bed, bogeymen in the closet and invasion of "bad guys" all stem from the same root: the idea that separating from us is terrifying. Nighttime fears are common in children, usually starting around three years of age and continuing until age six or so, and for children struggling with anxiety, nighttime fears can persist well into the later childhood years. According to Jocelynne Gordon and others, about one in three youth between the ages of eight and sixteen complains of these kinds of fears. It's especially important to avoid scary television shows, movies or stories right before bed; children's imaginations are revved up and filled with fantasy, which makes it difficult to separate fact from fiction.

Keep in mind that our children's fears are real to them. Forcing them to confront them because we're tired, or telling them to "be brave" isn't the answer. If common sense discussions about the difference between reality and fantasy don't work, we can tap in to their vivid imaginations to harness their fear. Using fear-fighting spray (page 115) to chase fear out the room, dream catchers to capture nightmares or a talisman to avert all things scary can help keep some kids' bedrooms monster-free. Giving our children the responsibility to look after their teddy or a pet can draw out their courage by transferring the fear to something else. A comment like, "Kitty is worried at nighttime. Can you take care of him tonight?" can be highly effective. If all else fails, we can remind kids that we and the adults in their lives are their ultimate protectors and that means keeping them safe at night. During my son's difficult sleep periods, I've even given him my scarf or sweater to nuzzle against, soothing him with my scent and signaling that I'm never far away.

The body-mind connection

Studies in neuroscience have shown a clear connection between physical activity and mental state. The findings make sense intuitively: we've all experienced feeling stronger, more energized and more mentally and emotionally clear after a little exercise. But exercise also has extraordinary benefits for children suffering from anxiety.

When our children are active, they're doing so much more than exercising their body; they're supporting the health of their brain. Bilateral movements, activities that use muscle systems on both sides of the body equally, integrate the two hemispheres of the brain and help our kids regain emotional balance. Information about the body's needs is processed more efficiently. Eventually kids feel more relaxed and clear. Under the right conditions, our bodies are self-healing systems that really do know how to find equilibrium.

Children with anxiety are frequently in a state of high alert, which means they produce and process large amounts of adrenaline and the stress hormone cortisol. Physical activity and exercise can reduce these stress hormones and increase the production of endorphins, the body's natural "feel-good" hormones. Research tells us that children who exercise regularly experience a significant decrease in their anxiety levels compared with those who are inactive. Exercise also improves our children's coordination, spatial skills, sleeping habits, focus and their overall health.

Fact: Researchers at the University of Illinois found that children who are more active and physically fit tend to have a bigger hippocampus and perform better on memory tests than their less-fit peers.

In response to this research on the importance of physical activity for brain development and neuroplasticity (the brain's ability to grow and change in response to stimuli), some schools in Vancouver, British Columbia, recently put into place a program that has made a remarkable difference in the classroom. Inspired by Active for Life (activeforlife.com), the Vancouver School Board encourages primary students to arrive at school fifteen minutes early for a "smart start." I was amazed when my son asked to be woken earlier so he could ride his bike to school to join in on dancing, kicking, running, throwing and other activities offered before classes. Teachers report that students who have taken part are more alert and show improved readiness to learn. Along with the physical and neurological benefits, there are social paybacks as well; the children form new bonds and create a better connection with their teachers.

Another way to build the mind-body connection is through organized sports. Activities such as soccer and martial arts can help kids develop self-confidence, a sense of accomplishment and interpersonal skills. Countless studies have shown that not only are athletes more likely to go to college, they also have better body image and are less likely to take up smoking or deal with depression or teen pregnancy. Of course, not all kids are keen on organized sports, especially kids who are fighting anxiety. When children are afraid or anxious about participating in group sports, it can be helpful to use a combination of cognitive restructuring tools (Getting to Know the Thinking Trap Culprits, page 85) and exposure techniques (Leveling Up and Out of Fear and Phobias, page 118), so they too can reap the developmental rewards and sense of connection organized sports provide.

In the meantime, activities like dodgeball, tag or even just running around the park are great ways to get moving. With a full family life, we're often so busy ferrying kids around to this or that activity that fitting in our own fitness regime becomes an afterthought. Make exercise a family activity. Imagine what we can accomplish together with a game of one-on-one basketball, a hike, a bicycle ride or even a simple game of catch in the front yard. Finding activities that we can share with our children builds the physical and emotional strength to keep us thriving. The goal here should be to help kids create a value system that puts activity high on the list of essential daily practices, right alongside getting good rest, spending time with family, learning new skills, caring for our nutrition, spending time in quiet reflection and playing with others.

Here are some fun, easy activities to do with children:

▸ **Scavenger hunts:** Looking for "treasure" can be a great way to get moving while having fun with the family, and the searches can be customized to any environment. My own kids love geocaching, a real-world outdoor treasure hunt done using a GPS (global positioning system) device. Imagine downloading the coordinates to find a geocache (container) at a hidden location, then tracking it using your GPS, signing the logbook to show you've met the goal and even trading a knick-knack you've brought for one in the geocache. The best news of all: there are over two million geocaches worldwide!

▸ **Obstacle courses:** Whether the challenges include running in a zig-zag, jumping over piles of pillows, climbing under a makeshift tunnel made with old sheets or walking with an egg on a spoon, obstacle courses are fun! Make them even more engaging by calling the obstacles part of superhero training school.

▸ **Yoga:** Yoga works every muscle in the body, is great for relaxation and teaches helpful breathing techniques. Its benefits to children with anxiety can't be overstated. Tuning in to the body and listening to all it's telling us is central to yoga. Once our children know how to squeeze their muscles into eagle pose or do downward dog, they're easily hooked.

▸ **Animal races:** Racing can be a lot of fun and it's an excellent way to get in some cardio time. The idea is to run like different animals from a starting point to the finish line. For younger children, divide the race into legs in which each competitor becomes a certain animal. Whether we are hopping like a rabbit or waddling like a duck, our hearts will be pumping and activating joy.

▸ **Clean-up races:** Cleaning up can be a great way to get in exercise, and it has the added benefit of restoring a room to a neat and tidy state. Set a timer or play a song to add an element of fun.

▸ **Mini-Olympics:** For a fun twist on playground time, create a mini-Olympics with homemade medals. Craft your own high jump, hurdles or discus (use a Frisbee) and you'll be well on your way to holding your own Summer Games. Don't forget to add the opening and closing ceremonies for extra fanfare!

▸ **Activity flash cards:** For days spent indoors, create activity flash cards to sneak some exercise into the day. Simply write some fun activities, such as "Do 10 jumping jacks" or "Crab crawl to the next room," on one side of the cards, then flip them over and draw the action on the back of the cards.

▸ **Video games:** Not all video games are for couch potatoes! Wii Fit has some great workout-themed games, from hula hooping to snowball fights, to get the blood pumping.

▸ **Pump up the jam sessions:** Get kids up and dancing. This is a great activity for an indoor day, and it gives our children a chance to share their favorite music with us.

ELEVEN

TWELVE STEPS TO HAPPINESS: AN ANXIETY ANTIDOTE

Nothing gives me more joy than talking about happiness, and there's a lot of happiness talk going around right now. There have been thousands of research studies about people who aren't doing well, but only recently have we begun to look at people who are thriving and ask, "What does it take to live with joy?" As parents, we also want to know how we can set our children on a path to lifelong happiness. I believe it's never too early for children to embrace the idea that they are amazing and powerful beings with all the inner resources they need to live a happy life. Happiness is the natural antidote to anxiety: where joy is present, anxiety cannot exist.

Positive psychology works towards understanding and promoting ways to make life more rewarding and fulfilling. Martin Seligman, a leading researcher in the field, gives us the formula in his book *Authentic Happiness*. He writes that around 50 percent of our potential for happiness lies within our genes, while 10 percent links to circumstances such as winning the lottery or experiencing a death in the family. A considerable 40 percent of our potential for happiness rests within our control. That means some children may have to work harder at feeling happy than others, but with a little commitment, it is within their reach. While we can't always easily change our circumstances, there are all kinds of voluntary variables that can improve how we feel about and look at life.

We are learning a great deal about how specific changes in our children's thinking and behaviors can help them to lead to healthier, happier lives. When children acquire some easily learned habits, they can find inner power and blossom into their most amazing self. It's all based on the fact that "the neurons that fire together, wire together." What that means is that the longer a particular set of neurons in our brain fires, the more deeply entrenched the related mental patterns become. Practicing good habits sets off fireworks of neural activity and encodes positive experiences into our children's neural structure. While some of the tools in this chapter may seem simple, they can have a powerful and positive effect. The more we help our children tune in to happiness, gratitude and the feeling that they are loved, successful and capable, the more they'll feel happy and less anxious.

Make a happiness plan

In his poem "Auguries of Innocence," William Blake wrote, "Joy and woe are woven fine." Certainly there is much to be learned when it comes to our children's pain, but while there is a time to soothe, there is also a time to support—and building a happiness plan can do just that. I'm not suggesting we set expectations for our children's mood—doing so could interfere with the development of their authentic self. But understanding the practices that can lead to authentic happiness can only help cultivate them in ourselves and our children.

THE HAPPINESS PLAN
Good for all ages
Materials needed: pens and paper, inspiring photo or magazine images
People who are happier overall believe that we can *choose* to be happy, and they make it a priority. Creating a happiness plan with our kids can help them to become more aware of the joy around them.

STEP 1: Start by talking to kids about the factors that influence their happiness quotient, emphasizing the whopping 40 percent that's within their control.

STEP 2: Help kids to compile a list of things that make them happy. This could include people they enjoy spending time with, music they like listening to and activities they find fun. Be sure to include simple things that they can do on their own, such as looking at family photos or thinking about an upcoming vacation. Anything goes, and there is no limit to the number of items on the list.

STEP 3: Post the list in a prominent place so it's easy for children to refer to any time they need a pick-me-up.

STEP 4: Help kids to choose three things from the list they want to do in the coming week to invite happiness in. Support them in planning how and when they think they will be able to do each thing. This doesn't have to be a schedule that they are forced to follow; it's more of an intention. If they aren't able to get to each thing, that's okay! Long-term happiness for children and adults alike relies on the regular use of healthy lifestyle and mindset practices.

Here are twelve other ideas that can make a positive difference to our children's mood and mindset.

1. CULTIVATE AN ATTITUDE OF GRATITUDE

There's a quote by Robert Holden, author of *Happiness Now!*, that I love. He tells us, "The real gift of gratitude is that the more grateful you are, the more present you become." Expressing gratitude is a tried-and-true route to feeling happier and more resilient and optimistic. According to a study in 2003 by Robert Emmons and Michael McCullough published in the *Journal of Personality and Social Psychology,* expressing gratitude also builds a better feeling about life overall and leads to fewer health complaints.

GRATITUDE VISIT

Good for all ages

Materials needed: pens, paper or a meaningful card

Dr. Martin Seligman has researched the impact of gratitude on happiness at length. He and his colleagues asked one group of participants to reflect on a time in their life when they were at their best and another group to make a "gratitude visit." Those who focused on gratitude reported a greater increase in happiness. Try this version of Dr. Seligman's gratitude visit.

STEP 1: Ask children to think of someone they'd like to thank for a gesture that meant a lot to them. Maybe that person helped out at a critical time, did something extraordinary or improved life for someone.

STEP 2: Help kids to write a letter of gratitude to the person. Encourage them to be specific about what the person did or said that they're grateful for and the impact it had on them.

STEP 3: Arrange to meet with the person and invite children to read the letter and share all the reasons why they appreciate this special person and what he or she has done.

GRATITUDE JOURNAL

Good for all ages

Materials needed: pens or markers and paper, an inspiring journal and photos

Dr. Seligman and his team also had individuals write down three things each day that went well for them and note the cause of the positive results. Those who participated every night for one week were happier and less depressed for the entire following month. Just imagine the effects if we were to commit to gratitude for a lifetime.

STEP 1: Invite children to think about how they've been feeling over the last week and rate their overall mood on their mood meter (page 76).

STEP 2: Help kids to start a journal dedicated to the things that are going well or that they're grateful for. Decorate it with photos and drawings. It only works if the gratitude is authentic, so keep in mind that less can be more. Include simple pleasures, and make sure they are meaningful. Children might also want to write about or draw pictures of the *cause* of the thing that went well in their life. Encourage them to write in this journal for one whole week, listing three good things per day.

STEP 3: After day seven, sit down with kids and ask them to point out where they feel on the mood meter now that the week is up. Help them compare their current state with their starting point. Unless something unusually difficult has happened in the past week, most kids will find that their mood meter score has improved.

2. PRACTICE NOT-SO-RANDOM ACTS OF KINDNESS

Acts of kindness and reaching out to those in need can lift our mood and provide a sense of purpose. Small acts, such as helping a grandparent or reading to a younger child, can help our children too. With this strategy, more really *is* better; random acts are especially beneficial when repeated at least five times a week.

Why do acts of altruism make children feel so good about themselves? It seems these acts not only make children feel more connected with others, they also shift focus away from themselves, which can provide valuable relief from anxious thought patterns. Research also suggests that variety is key; rather than repeating the same act of kindness over and over which can cause it to lose its effect, encourage children to come up with lots of small acts they can do.

THE KINDNESS LIST

Good for all ages

Materials needed: pens and paper or a journal

This is one exercise that has very little downside to trying it out, while the opportunity to engage children's hearts is priceless. Sit down together and create a "kindness list" of things that kids could do to help or show kindness to someone they care about. Try to act on them as often as possible throughout the week, perhaps even daily—motivation, frequency and variety are the secret formula for success here. Record these acts of kindness together in a journal or display them proudly on a blackboard. Make sure to participate too!

3. EMBRACE THE POWER OF "LESS"

From the grocery store to television, it feels as if we have more options to choose from all the time. Dr. Seligman points out the paradox of modern life is that rather than bringing us greater fulfillment, having too many options can leave us feeling dissatisfied. His research tells us that when children have to pick the "best choice" out of a wide selection, they often feel more pessimistic, stressed, tired, anxious and, in the end, disappointed. However, if we teach children that sometimes good enough is good enough, they are able to derive more satisfaction from what's available. Teaching our kids to try our best but not sweat the small stuff (and truly living it ourselves) leads to greater happiness for the whole family.

4. SMILE

Ever notice that when we're feeling crummy, if we turn up the corners of our mouth into a smile, something magical starts to happen—we feel better. Smiling triggers positive memories, while thinking of something positive makes us smile in return. Some researchers theorize that how our facial muscles are arranged can create temperature changes in the brain. For example, a scared face signals we're in danger, so our brain tells our heart to work harder, increasing our pulse and body temperature. When we make a scared face, the brain warms up and soon we become ready to protect ourselves from danger. When we smile, the brain relaxes and becomes cooler. And, the cooler temperature actually triggers happiness!

While a smile can improve our mood, it's important to "keep it real." Forced smiling can actually worsen our mood. To stimulate genuine smiles, try placing pictures of silly, delightful or beloved people, things and events in kids' school agenda or coat pocket, on the refrigerator and in any other place where they'll encounter them regularly.

5. LAUGH IT UP

The short- and long-term benefits of laughter are well proven: a good laugh lightens our load both mentally and physically. Think about everything our body experiences while we are guffawing about something silly. We take in more oxygen; our heart, stomach muscles and lungs become stimulated; and endorphins are released. Not only that, the increase in blood circulation through-out the body triggers a relaxation response. Beyond the physical benefits, moments of laughing with our children can also build a connection that will help cut through feelings of anxiety.

GIGGLE MILKSHAKE

Good for all ages

Materials needed: none

When things aren't going the way we've planned and everything seems to be upside down, we sometimes need a good giggle to help us re-energize. Going over all the changes in our body that come with laughing can help explain to kids why it's so beneficial. Encourage them to fill up with giggles just by using their imagi-nation. You can even do it together.

STEP 1: Ask kids to start by holding out their hands as if they're holding a glass. Tell them it's their special milkshake glass, and they can use it to drink their very own milkshake made of giggles. It can be any color, any shape and any size they choose. Encourage them to think about the glass—how it feels and looks in their hands.

STEP 2: Now ask them to fill up their special glass with as many silly, funny thoughts as they can think of. Remember all the funny times they've had with family and friends or all the funny things they've seen. Remind them of their favorite funny jokes and the things that make their belly fill up with laughter. Then gather up those thoughts, mix them together and pour all those thoughts into their milkshake glass.

STEP 3: Once all of those thoughts are contained in the glass, ask kids to put a lid on top of the glass and shake. Shake, shake it as hard as they can to get those funny thoughts all stirred up together.

STEP 4: Once their thoughts are all mixed up, it's time to drink up. Stick in a straw and drink that funny milkshake and let the silly thoughts fill their tummy. Then let the laughter out and let it travel all over their body!

> **PARENTING TIP:** Collect pictures, comics and jokes your children find funny as a way to trigger their laughter response.

5. STRIVE FOR GOALS

Having a goal and working steadily towards it doesn't just teach our children mastery, it can also lead to greater happiness. Neuroscientists tell us that hard work and the satisfaction of realizing a goal will activate positive feelings while suppressing fear and other negative emotions. Although working at a difficult skill, such as playing a musical instrument, building a go-kart or kicking a field goal, can elevate stress and anxiety in the short term, mastery over time leads to a sense of satisfaction and happiness. Help children choose a goal that resonates for *them,* as this will further ignite a sense of ownership and autonomy and make their efforts more gratifying.

DREAM MAP
Good for all ages
Materials needed: felt pens and paper, photo images that symbolize the goal or dream
Look for an opening to talk with children about their biggest dreams. They may be different from what we might expect, and it can be tough to restrain our impulse to direct them. Instead, be curious. When we respect their hopes and let them know that we are interested in their dreams and invite them to imagine what it would look like to achieve those goals, we create a sense of possibility. How would it feel? What would they be doing, thinking and saying?

STEP 1: Have kids choose one dream, and help them to create a timeline showing all the steps along the path to that dream. Make sure to create mini-goals along the way to increase the sense of accomplishment. For example, if our children's ultimate dream is to become a fashion designer and they have taken to decorating T-shirts, take the next step. Get curious and ask what attracts them to fashion design, whether they have a fashion design role model and what the next step might be on their fashion design path. Once we've fully entered into their world, we can help guide them to a specific goal and some mini-goals.

STEP 2: Make time to help kids work towards their goals. Perhaps, we can find a fashion mentor to create masterpieces with them, plan a fashion show or sell their creations at a craft fair. Maybe we can make an appointment to sit down together every Sunday morning to sketch creations and sew.

STEP 3: Check in on the timeline every now and again to look back on where they started and see how far they've come and adjust the original plan, as required. Keep in mind, sometimes the goal changes as you learn more about it (and yourself!)—you want to learn the sax rather than the clarinet—or you unexpectedly discover a bigger passion—photography rather than fashion design.

Making progress towards a goal and mastering a talent step by step feels good and provides opportunities for our kids to discover how capable they are.

6. LISTEN TO HAPPY MUSIC
Listening to positive music can lift our children's spirits, and actively trying to feel happier while doing it is even more potent. A study by Yuna Ferguson and Kennon Sheldon, published in

the *Journal of Positive Psychology,* had participants listen to uplifting music, and those who put conscious effort into feeling happier while listening by focusing on positive thoughts had the highest level of positive mood in the end. The purposeful mindset is key, whether listening to uplifting music, flashing an authentic smile or taking note of what we're grateful for. Making a conscious decision towards thoughts and actions that bring in happiness creates an imprint on the brain that can last for life. Add a little singing and dancing to the mix, and the positive feelings will soar even higher. Here's a list of songs that make me happy and put me and my kids in a good mood, but add to this list or create your own with your children, according to what moves you.

Happiness Playlist
"Happy"—Pharrell Williams
"I'm On My Way"—The Proclaimers
"Let It Go"—Idina Menzel
"Best Day of My Life"—American Authors
"Hakuna Matata"—The Lion King
"I Feel Good"—James Brown
"Behind The Clouds"—Brad Paisley
"Bring it All Back"—S Club 7
"Man In The Mirror"—Michael Jackson
"Lean On Me"—Bill Withers
"We're All in This Together"—High School Musical
"Here Comes The Sun"—The Beatles

7. PLAY WITH A FURRY FRIEND
This is some happiness homework most children will easily buy into: spend some time with a pet. One study by Dognition, an organization founded by Duke University researcher and cognitive scientist Brian Hare, found pet ownership to be strongly

connected to increased well-being. Researchers found that the act of petting a dog decreases blood pressure and increases dopamine, prolactin and oxytocin, hormones associated with happiness and bonding, as well as beta-endorphins, which are associated with euphoria and pain relief. Snuggling a furry friend causes a pleasure surge on a par with finding money, eating chocolate and looking at pictures of smiling babies.

A study by Allen McConnell of Miami University found that pet owners feel better about themselves. They are also less lonely and fearful, more physically active, conscientious and extroverted than those who don't own pets. Don't have a pet? Consider co-parenting a friend's pet. Try dog sitting, giving a pet owner a day off or building a regular visitation or dog-walking schedule. Or try volunteering at the pet rescue shelters in the area. Blending volunteer work with animal bonding is especially powerful since both are shown to bolster happiness.

8. DELIGHT IN THE SMALL STUFF

According to neuropsychologist Rick Hanson, our brains have an in-built bias for negativity, which puts us on high alert for *the bad* in life. As he describes it, "The brain is like Velcro for negative experiences and Teflon for positive ones." One way to counteract this tendency is to take notice of the small positives in everyday moments. Letting our children know that the secret to happiness could be as simple as paying attention can help them turn up their curiosity dial. The more they tune in to small wonders, the more they will strengthen their positivity muscle. It can be helpful to give our own examples and model what we're after. For example, we might say, "I love this cup of tea" or "This music makes me so happy." Invite children to turn the spotlight of their mind towards the little thing they've decided to delight in for one whole mindful minute. Throughout the day, we can set a "timer" for mindful moments and notice our children's spotlight moving away from the thoughts that get them down and towards those that lift them up.

9. FIND HAPPINESS IN TOGETHERNESS

Close relationships and a sense of connectedness are perhaps our most valuable buffers against life's ups and downs. Evidence shows that they increase our immune functioning and lower health risks overall. Both the quality and quantity of social connection factor into the effect; at the top of the list are sharing positive emotions and experiences, giving and receiving support and feeling understood.

On average, people living in small towns are happier than those who live in big cities, primarily due to one key factor—community. Support systems are key. Chatting with a neighbor, getting to know the local grocer and giving and receiving support with family and friends are all ways in which we benefit from our connections with other people. For children, Mom and Dad come first. When children feel emotionally supported by our focused support, happiness is a natural by-product. And when we delight in being with our children, we are basking in the most rewarding connection of all.

Fact: Engaging in more meaningful conversation can actually result in higher levels of happiness! A study by Matthias Mehl found that people who spent more time talking to other people about topics they were passionate about reported higher levels of happiness than people who engaged in small talk. It's not about how much you talk but what you talk about!

COMMUNITY WEB
Good for all ages
Materials needed: pens, paper and geometry compass or traceable circles
This is a helpful tool when we might be feeling lonely, to remember how many people we know—and how many more people we come into contact with and could get to know!

STEP 1: Start by asking children if they've ever noticed how many people they come across in their day. Help them to brainstorm a list of names of people they know, as well as descriptions of strangers they come into contact with regularly but don't yet know personally.

STEP 2: On a large sheet of paper, draw six concentric "tribe circles." Have children put themselves in the center circle. The next circle includes family members, and the others are friends, acquaintances, community members and strangers.

STEP 3: Invite children to put the names or drawings of people into each category, exploring together what each person means to them. Some people move in and out of categories from time to time, but all play an important part in the community web.

STEP 4: Ask children who they would like to get to know better and make a plan that will help them do that.

10. GET A MOVE ON
In chapter 9, we learned that our body and mind are inseparable. The latest studies from a team of researchers at Duke University led by Michael Babyak add fuel to the argument that exercise can fend off depression and calm anxieties as well as protect against the harmful physical consequences of stress. Along with their health benefits, walking to school and chasing around the jungle

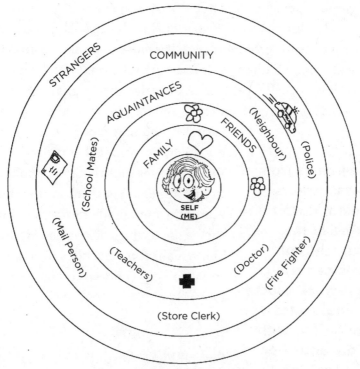

COMMUNITY WEB

gym are great ways to increase happiness. Studies show we're happier when we're in natural environments than when we are indoors, and walking tall leads to improved mood after only three minutes. Test the science behind getting a move on by having kids check their mood meter before and after being active, and they'll better understand the powerful connection between the two.

11. MEDITATE

New curricula and parenting books have brought mindfulness out of New Age retreats and Buddhist temples and into the common language in schools and homes. Mindfulness practice is a movement well supported by brain research, and it shows that finding one's spiritual center and using meditation as a technique to do so has far-reaching benefits. It can lower our stress levels, improve our sleep and boost our overall emotional well-being. All it requires is sitting and quieting the mind (which is much easier said than done!).

Persuading children to sit in contemplation for any period of time can be a challenge. Here is one trick that might help. Invite kids to sit on an imaginary train. Tell them to close their eyes and turn their internal spotlight on the scenery going by. Notice that the scenery is full of images and thoughts about caring for others. Ask them to do a body scan and notice where in their body they sense feelings of love and kindness. The visualization exercises in chapter 6 can also help children to enter a meditative state.

Fact: A team of researchers from Massachusetts General Hospital looked at the brain scans of participants in an eight-week course in mindfulness meditation, both before and after the class. The study concluded that parts of the participants' brains associated with compassion and self-awareness had grown and parts associated with stress had shrunk by the end of the course.

12. PRAY

Several hundred studies have put spirituality front and center as a primary reason we feel happier, heal faster, are healthier overall and cope better with life's challenges. While going to mass, temple or synagogue may not be first on our list after a long day at work or with the kids, it can be a great way to bust stress and boost happiness. The research of Dr. Harold Koenig from Duke University is compelling. In his survey of more than a thousand studies, he found that heart patients without spiritual beliefs were fourteen times more likely to die following surgery; elderly people without spiritual beliefs were at twice the risk for stroke; hospitalized people who didn't attend church stayed in hospital three times longer and people who had religious affiliation became depressed less often and recovered more quickly.

What exactly is so powerful about religious connections? Social connectedness and a hopeful mindset are likely to be the strongest factors in improving well-being. Giving and getting support, combined with faith that we are part of a greater whole, go a long way towards bolstering our peace of mind, our body, and for those in the divinity camp, our peace of spirit.

Celebrate uniqueness

A huge part of our personal happiness springs from our feelings about ourselves. When we understand ourselves, approve of ourselves and even accept our quirks and vulnerabilities, we are more resilient and less prone to seeking validation from other people. Strengthening our children's sense of their unique qualities will help them to grow in self-awareness and self-acceptance. By reserving the right to define themselves on their own terms, they can remain personally powerful for life.

THE POWER OF A PERSONAL MOTTO
Good for all ages
Materials needed: none

Social media is full of oodles of quotes from the great minds in history. Some are meant to inspire; others, provoke thought or simply amuse. The power of a personal mantra or motto is in the clarity of the message; the brain is able to cut through all the mental clutter and get straight to the point. Neuroscientists have shown how the age-old practice of repeating mantras affects the brain. When we think positively, cortisol levels decrease and serotonin levels improve, which increase our sense of well-being. The simple act of stating powerful words can actually change our body's physiology and consciousness.

STEP 1: Let children know that the most powerful leaders in the world usually have a personal motto to remind them of what matters most when life gets confusing or hard. The Dalai Lama reminds himself, "Choose to be optimistic, it feels better," while Winston Churchill said, "Continuous effort—not strength or intelligence—is the key to unlocking our potential." These are powerful words to live by.

STEP 2: Invite children to read through the examples of personal mottos below, then choose one or create one of their own.

1. "Some days you just have to create your own sunshine."
2. "You're off to Great Places! Today is your day! Your mountain is waiting, so . . . get on your way."—Dr. Seuss
3. "She turned her can'ts into cans and her dreams into plans." —Kobi Yamada
4. "Can't stop. Won't stop."
5. "Live. Laugh. Love."
6. "Never stop trying."
7. "Today you are You. That is truer than true. There is no one alive who is Youer than You."—Dr. Seuss
8. "Don't cry because it's over. Smile because it happened." —Dr. Seuss
9. "Today was good. Today was fun. Tomorrow is another one."—Dr. Seuss
10. "You've always had the power."—*The Wizard of Oz*
11. "Positive mind. Positive vibes. Positive life."
12. "What you tell yourself every day will either lift you up or tear you down."
13. "Be in the now."
14. "I am stronger than this challenge. And this challenge is making me even stronger."

15. "Be strong enough to stand alone, smart enough to know when you need help and brave enough to ask for it."
16. "It's not who you are that holds you back, it's who you think you're not."
17. "If it doesn't challenge you, it won't change you."
18. "When you think about quitting, think about why you started."
19. "If you can dream it, you can do it."—Walt Disney

> **PARENTING TIP:** Have kids change or update their personal motto from time to time—and don't forget to put that motto in all kinds of places to help them remember it. Try putting it on a T-shirt with fabric pens, or making an infographic on the computer. And, sharing a personal motto of our own shows our children that we all need a little inspiration now and again.

MISSION STATEMENT—A DECLARATION OF AWESOME

Best for ages 7–12

Materials needed: paper and markers

Companies have been pinpointing their underlying values and crystallizing their mission statements for decades. They know a clear, compelling vision can inspire their workers and guide them to their destination. For children with anxiety, recognizing strengths, talents and positive values can be a struggle. But creating their own mission statement, or "declaration of awesome," gives them a plan to keep them on track as they work towards their goals. This declaration is not set in stone; it can change and evolve as our children acquire new skills and grow from new experiences. Have everyone in the family generate their own declaration of awesome to better understand each other.

STEP 1: Start by letting children know how important it is to stop our busy lives from time to time and remember all the good stuff we believe in and what we appreciate about ourselves. Offer to interview them so you can make a "declaration of awesome" to show all the cool aspects of who they already are. For younger children, make the exercise playful by using a toy microphone or digital recorder and inviting them to be interviewed on a "radio show." There are no hard and fast rules when creating the declaration. Answer as many or as few questions as seem relevant.

1. Describe when you think you feel your best. What does that look like? Who are you with and what are doing?
2. Describe what you really love doing at school, at work, at dance class, at gymnastics. What gets you excited about the activities you do during the day? What about things you enjoy doing at home with your family?
3. What are your talents and natural gifts?
4. Are you an artist? Can you draw and paint really well? Or are you more of a musician? Do you have an instrument you love to play? Are you a great friend, or very good at making decisions and helping out?
5. If you had all the time and money in the world, what would you choose to do?
6. What do you think you contribute to the lives of the people around you?
7. What are some things that you would like to change or do in the future?
8. Name five qualities that best describe you.
9. What are things that you do to take care of yourself? How do you recharge your brain so it's ready to take on a new day? What do you accept about yourself?

STEP 2: Now, help children create their personal mission statement by narrowing down their core values of who they are, what is important to them and what inspires them. The result should be concise—just a few sentences—and incorporate their core elements. For example, "Liam loves hockey more than anything else in the world and wants to be a goalie when he grows up. He is an awesome big brother and loves reading to his little sister, Caitlin. Liam is generous and funny and likes to make people laugh! When Liam gets tired, he speeds up instead of slowing down, and his favorite way to relax is by doing the Forest Visualization with his mom."

STEP 3: Display the Declaration of Awesome in a prominent place to say, "This is what I'm all about."

CARE TAG

Good for all ages

Materials needed: paper and pens

Just like our clothes, we can all use a reminder of how we like to be treated and cared for. It's like having special care instructions for our hearts and minds. A good way to remind us of this is to spend some time to create our very own personal care tags.

What might we need to take care of our emotions, our body and brain? We can create some symbols that represent our child's personal care instructions and add all the things they like to do every day to feel in charge of themselves! Have them draw the symbols on a poster or sheet of paper and display it in their bedroom or playroom to remind them of the importance of daily self-care. Care items might include:

1. Breathing mindfully
2. Doing progressive relaxation
3. Listening to happy music
4. Taking a fear-fighting step
5. Checking the amygdala or mood meter
6. Doing a visualization
7. Doing a thought buster
8. Looking at family photos
9. Drawing pictures
10. Writing in a journal
11. Having a bubble bath
12. Playing a board game
13. Going for a bike ride
14. Having cuddle time
15. Making a healthy snack
16. Reading my motto
17. Reading my mission statement

In the end, we all want our children to be the fullest expression of themselves—happy, thriving and free from serious problems. But adversity isn't the enemy of happiness. It's through learning to cope with life's natural ups and downs that we enrich ourselves with wisdom and adaptability.

The message throughout this book has been that we can create the reality we dream of for our children by fostering the kind of environment that naturally allows them to thrive. At any given moment, we have the power to choose two possible futures: one in which we hold on to old patterns and one in which we stretch towards change. Our good parenting instincts, self-awareness and ability to connect deeply with our children will allow everyday experiences to become teaching moments. The play-based CBT, positive psychology and brain science tools in this book can transform daily parenting challenges into moments of fun and resilience.

Through this approach, our children will develop the confidence they need to meet anxiety head on and know they can cope and thrive in the most difficult of situations.

Time and time again, I have found that when, as parents, we commit to positive change and integrate these self-awareness tools into our daily lives, the whole family benefits in long-lasting ways. Children who develop this heightened self-insight have the profound ability to soothe both their mind and body and ultimately discover greater happiness and meaning in their lives. Their learning ability will soar and their relationship with themselves, their family and community will become stronger. Understanding their brain system, tuning up their internal awareness and making big and small shifts in their choices and behavior can all change the direction of their development, as each stage sets a healthy foundation for the next. It can be encouraging to imagine our children as teens with a well-developed ability to monitor their own well-being, knowing deeply that they are in control of their thoughts, feelings and actions. They will have conditioned themselves to approach difficult and opposing emotions with curiosity and compassion rather than hardening against them. This remarkable internal acuity will remain their best defense against life's greatest challenges, even into adulthood. And we will have ultimately learned transformative lessons through our sacred parent-child bond.

It's my hope that the fundamental message of resilience and connection within these pages provides a foundation of support for intentional and connected parenting, reminding us that our contribution matters deeply. And with all the mistakes we will inevitably make as parents and all the situations we cannot control, our ability to stay present and come together as a family will see us through the ups and downs.

Anxiety tells us that we are alone or insufficient. Stress tells us that our problems are larger than ourselves. Struggling with these powerful emotions without support in a culture of disconnect can make us feel overwhelmed and defeated. By honoring ourselves, being consciously aware of our children's emotional reality, trusting in their ability to overcome their challenges and giving them the tools to do so, we can use the power of our parenting as an agent for change, connection and powerful positivity that will last a lifetime.

INDEX

ACKNOWLEDGMENTS

I'm grateful to be working at a time when there is great attention to the needs of children and families, and I'm equally grateful to have many colleagues who take it as the purpose of their spirit to inspire deeper insight and understanding. I stand on the shoulders of great thinkers and particularly wish to acknowledge the depth of learning and support I have received from Dr. John Allan; for two decades, he has been unwavering in his compassionate guidance.

It doesn't escape me that so much of my joy in writing this book is thanks to the heartfelt work of a team of clinicians and students who have contributed a great deal of knowledge, insight and creativity to a topic for which we share a deep commitment. Liana Yip, Alyssa Bauman (nourished.ca), Natasha Saini, Stephanie Mather and Myriame Lyons have worked with hundreds of children, fine-tuning and redesigning the concepts and activities to ensure they truly accomplish the heart of their purpose. And to Jamie Lynn, your steady and capable presence has been deeply reassuring and truly invaluable.

Without the brave families and children who have allowed me to enter their world in times of great vulnerability, this book would not exist. I'm honored that you have trusted in me.

To my editor, Maggie Langrick, thank you for creating an opening of transformation through the writing of this book, and for your belief in me as a first-time book author.

And to my family and friends, through your sustenance you open me up to possibility and a faith that anything can be accomplished.